DELHI

HISTORICAL GLIMPSES

DELHI
HISTORICAL GLIMPSES

R.V. SMITH

ARYAN BOOKS INTERNATIONAL
New Delhi

∞⦰↗

Dedicated to my late cousin, Adeline Lall,
wife of Dr. T.D. Lall and foundress of
St. Mary's schools, New Delhi,
who helped to enrich the
cultural life of the Capital.

⸺

DELHI: HISTORICAL GLIMPSES

ISBN: 978-81-7305-369-6

First published in **2010** by
ARYAN BOOKS INTERNATIONAL
Pooja Apartments, 4B, Ansari Road, New Delhi-110 002 (India)
Tel.: 23287589, 23255799; Fax: 91-11-23270385
E-mail: aryanbooks@vsnl.com, aryanbooks@gmail.com

Computer Typeset and Printed in India at
ABI Prints & Publishing Co., New Delhi

Preface

This book on Delhi gives the facets of a historical city, with its monuments and the legends connected with it. Where else could one find a better dwelling place for Clio than the 'eternal Capital', which is as old as history itself and at par with the Luxor of the pharaohs and the Athens of the Greeks? Most of the contents, however, are related to the medieval period, though you will find scattered references to the dim past peeping out of the crust of latter-day events. Delhi lures the heart like a beloved who can never be forgotten – affectionate no doubt, but a proud entity who cannot be the mistress of anyone, no matter how great and powerful. One is supposed to just admire her many nuances down the memory lane and take her to heart, if not to bed.

These articles, the labour of many years, have appeared in the 'Down Memory Lane' and 'Quaint Corner' columns of *The Hindu* and *The Statesman*, with sketches by my son Tony. My heartfelt gratitude to the two newspapers and to my father, the late Thomas Smith, who inculcated in my brothers and me an intense love for history, particularly in the Golden Triangle comprising Delhi, Agra and Jaipur. Perhaps some of our infatuation may get rubbed on to the reader too!

Mayapuri, New Delhi   **R.V. Smith**

Contents

PRE-MOGHUL PERIOD

1

Forgotten Medieval 'New Delhi'

Near South Extension Part-I lies Kotla Mubarakpur in which is situated the tomb of Mubarak Shah, the second of the Sayyid kings. It is a neglected place now with vandalism and unauthorized constructions making it a veritable rabbit's warren. But while the 15th century was still in its third decade, it was the site selected for a 'New Delhi' by Mubarak Shah, who wanted to enshrine his name in the galaxy of great builders. He had ascended the throne after Khizr Khan, who had been given the freedom of Lahore and Multan by Taimur.

Khizr Khan had been waiting for an opportunity to seize Delhi and when Mahmud Tughlak died he started making preparations to install himself as the next king. In 1414 he took advantage of the anarchy in North India to achieve his heart's desire and started the Sayyid dynasty. But after a short reign of seven years Khizr Khan died and Mubarak Shah became king.

Mubarak Shah ruled from 1421 to 1434, when he was murdered at Mubarakabad, as it was then known, at the behest of Sarvar-ul-Mulk, the ousted Minister of Revenue. It was a Friday afternoon, just before the 'Juma prayers', when the unlucky Mubarak was struck down with impunity. He was succeeded by two other Sayyid kings, the last of whom was forced to retire to Badaon by Bahlol Lodhi, founder of the Lodhi dynasty.

An octagonal wall once enclosed Mubarak Shah's tomb. But now the wall and many other buildings have disappeared, leaving only a gate on the south and a mosque on the west. It is through the southern gate that one enters the mausoleum. Coloured plaster (now peeling off) and inscriptions from the *Koran* decorate the ceiling of the main dome. The monument is a fine example of Indo-Islamic architecture and the octagonal tombs popularized by the Sayyids. In course of time this pattern was followed by both the Lodhis and the Moghuls, Adham Khan's tomb, built in Mehrauli during Akbar's reign, being an outstanding example.

Many of the monuments of the Sayyid period are to be found in Kherpur village, now known as Lodhi Gardens. Among these is the tomb of Mohammad Sayyid, Mubarak Shah's successor. Closer to Mubarakpur is the Teen Burji, or three tombs, the largest of which forms the last resting place of Khizr Khan.

Mubarak Shah's reign of 13 years, three months and 16 days ended on January 4, 1434 but gave birth to a new style of architecture. Today Kotla Mubarakpur is a poor cousin of the fashionable South Extension and is still classified as a village, where Juma prayers are a reminder that man was created on a Thursday and his final judgement on *Qayamat* will be on a Friday afternoon, just about the time that Mubarak Shah was murdered. That's a belief flavoured by local lore.

2

Tomb of a Genius – Amir Khusrau

Standing outside the tomb of Amir Khusrau, eating *khichra* and breathing the aroma of joss sticks and rose water, one is transported from the narrow confines of Delhi's Bustee Nizamuddin to the 13th century when this prince of poets was at the peak of his popularity. Khusrau, handsome and witty, was just as much at home at the royal court as at the "*panghat* of the village well where the belles were amazed by his wisdom".

Khusrau was a great traveller but Turkey, Iran and Afghanistan did not attract him so much as his beloved Hindustan where his natural intelligence blossomed. He served several kings during an eventful life but devotion to Hazrat Nizamuddin made him return to the saint's *Khanqah* (abode) again and again.

A royal spy passing through the *bustee* once remarked:

I heard that you were laughing at a village well in Etah the other day and today you are returing from the *Khanqah* of the dervish with piety dripping from your face.

Khusrau smiled and said,

The belles at the *panghat* give me water to drink and *kheer* to relish after a hard day's journey. If I coin riddles for them they find a pleasant deversion. They giggle when they come to know that the solution was as simple as *kheer*, and I laugh with them. But now after visiting the *Auliya* I have felt a different pleasure and you naturally see piety on my face.

Whether the spy was convinced is not known but as you finish the *khichra* with your tongue afire, you also think of *kheer* and the riddle coined by the nobleman.

Hazrat Nizamuddin Auliya as Khusrau's friend, guide and philosopher had such a profound influence on the man who came to be known as 'Tooti-e-Hind' that the names of the two are inter-linked. The *tooti* is a small songbird and like it, Khusrau kept enchanting everybody all his life. Born at Patiali in Etah district (UP), in 1253, the poet died soon after Hazrat Nizamuddin in 1326. He uttered his famous lines, "Gori soye sej pe mukh pe dale kesh" and became mum. A classic case of a man dying of a broken heart.

The monument to the east of the Nizamuddin *dargah* is the last resting place of the genius who excelled in many fields and was later exalted to sainthood himself. They still hold an annual Urs (death anniversary function) at his grave but the best time to visit it is in the afternoon when the *khichra* is still fresh and there are fewer distractions for those comtemplating Khusrau's wit and humour, the one who saw "the light that never was on sea or land/the consecration and the poet's dream" long before Wordsworth.

3

Lost Ambience of Hauz Khas

When Taimur the Lame camped on the bank of Hauz Khas in 1398, his historian Sharfuddin Yazdi remarked that the place was not only a good retreat, but worthy of respect for its creator, whom he wrongly thought was Firoz Shah Tughlak. The tank was actually built by Alauddin Khilji, who reigned from 1296 to 1316. Firoz added to the complex. At that time Taimur had just defeated Mahmud Tughlak and was gloating over his victory, but he did have an eye for architecture.

Students of history will recall that after his return to Samarqand, Amir Taimur built many majestic edifices, including a famous mosque with the help of the artisans he had taken from India. But there was one which was the brainchild of his begum, who was very beautiful, indeed. When the monument was completed she was overjoyed because the architect had been able to give concrete shape to her dream edifice. It was early evening when she went to view it all alone and asked the architect what reward she could give him for the masterpiece. The man replied that the reward was beyond her. The begum's curiosity aroused, she asked him to name it and that it would be his. The masterbuilder hesitated and then whispered, 'A kiss'.

The begum looked at the man, not a handsome one at all. But even so she thought he deserved it and nodded assent. The shadows were lengthening when the architect (was he also from India?) took the begum in his arms and kissed her with such passion that he left a black mark on her cheek. "Sweet Helen, make me immortal with a kiss," said Faustus to the apparition of Helen of Troy that he had conjured up. But in the case of the architect the request worked the other way round, for instead of immortality he got death. The spies had seen it all and Taimur's vengeance followed. But the begum carried that black mark on her cheek as long as

History in ruins

she lived. However, the monument on which her fame rests is the one built by the unfortunate architect, though according to one version he did not have to pay with his life after all.

Back to Hauz Khas. That evening in 1398, Taimur enjoyed the sunset over Delhi, for it was the best site in the capital to do so even as late as the 1960s. The British too had felt the same way. One heard the song, *Jab shaam dhale aana, Jab deep jalen aanaa* sung by Yesudas in that setting at sundown many years ago and the echo is still heard deep in the heart even in the mundane surroundings of Hauz Khas.

The mod Hauz Khas village seems to be the culprit. Ever since it came up the monument has lost its sanctity. The village that had co-existed with the monument for centuries has vanished and in its place have come up shops, restaurants, boutiques and what not. The neo-rich flaunt their affluence at a place where once "the plowman homeward plod his weary way" and instead of the "lowing herd" there are cars aplenty parked right up to the monument, so much so that one finds it difficult to make one's way to it.

The high prices offered to the villagers made them sell both their lands and ancestral homes. Now nobody seems to be able to enforce any order or discipline. According to the Conservation Society, Delhi, while the monument is under the charge of the Archaeological Survey of India, the ground surrounding it is the DDA's which means right up to the steps of Hauz Khas. Though the ASI maintains the monument proper it cannot do anything about the surroundings.

A strange state of affairs, indeed!

Hauz Khas was excavated by Alauddin after a dream in which he saw the hoof of the Prophet's steed strike a piece of ground and water flow out from it. The dream took the shape of a tank, Hauz-e-Alai, to meet the needs of the inhabitants of the second city of Delhi, Siri, which he founded in 1304.

In 1354, Firoz Tughlak desilted the Hauz and built several buildings around it in an L-shaped pattern covering the entire 70-acre area. He also built a double-storeyed *madarsa* with colonnades and residential quarters for students and teachers. The rubble-built tomb of Firoz Tughlak is also there in the form of a plastered square chamber. Buried alongside are the emperor's second son and grandson. The entrance is through an eastern door. In 1507 Sikandar Lodhi repaired the tomb. And at one time the villagers grew crops over the dry tank.

Now, thanks to the new Hauz Khas village, much of the beauty of the place is lost and evenings do not come there as coyly as they used to when earthen lamps were lit and a mellow voice courted the beloved in a song.

4

Glazed Mystery in Dome

On a traffic island, a road from which leads to Humayun's Tomb, stands Sabz Burj with its magnificent dome of glazed tiles. One wonders who built it and to commemorate what? That it is pre-Moghul is evident, but the story behind it is missing. Gazing at the monument, given a facelift by the Archaeological Survey of India, one gets a string of ideas as to its identity.

Was it once built in the centre of a garden which disappeared over the centuries? Perhaps some king, fond of the outdoors, surveyed nature from under the shade of this dome – in winter, spring, summer and in the rainy season when the clouds of *Sawan* burst forth to bestow the life-giving showers on a parched and thirsty land. Were there fountains here once which played high into the trees? Where have all the flowers gone which bloomed in those times? If the road around the monument were to be dug up, could one find ancient or medieval waterways, like the ones dating back to Babar's times discovered under fields and villages in Rajasthan by Mrs. Moynihan, the wife of a former US Ambassador to India?

Perhaps Sabz Burj was not a garden tower, but a memorial to a woman, a beautiful one, who had stolen the heart of an emperor or a noble, or a general, drunk with the glory of his conquests? Or of a prince who had access to his father's treasury and fulfilled every whim of a wife or mistress? Could the *burj* have been the creation of an empress during the lifetime, or after the death, of her all-powerful husband? What did she look like, this nameless woman? A Muslim for sure, fair, tall and slender and clothed in silks, with jewelled bangles tinkling at her wrists and anklets at her feet, a pearl necklace around her dainty neck, her nose decorated with a nosegay of some precious stone that twinkled in the moonlight, her golden *cummuerbund* dangling from a narrow waist, her curvaceous body moving in rhythm as she walked with graceful steps, her comely face partly visible through a flimsy veil!

Could it be that Subz Burj had nothing to do with a woman but a mendicant, who blessed the mighty and whose memory was perpetuated by them? There are hermits who are considered *Sada Suhag* (always in nuptial bliss). They are men, of course, but regard themselves as feminine in spirit and as such betrothed to God. These dervishes wear not only green clothes, but also green bangles (as a sign of their evergreen love divine) and dress like women, with long hair, and pigtails too. A memorial tower to such a one would be *sabz* (green) no doubt.

A peculiarity of this monument is the use of glazed green tiles on the dome and drum. Could these have given the name to it? If so, where did the tiles come from in that distant age and what was their significance? Even Sir Sayyid Ahmed Khan, such an authority on Delhi's past, is silent about this edifice. We can only fall back on conjectures then and hope that the monument after its renovation (unfortunately blue tiles have been used) would continue to baffle the passerby, like an ageless woman on the crossroads attracting a thousand glances and the sighs that go with them.

5

Ship-Shaped Palace

A palace shaped like a ship, that's Jahaz Mahal in Mehrauli. The *mahal* is located on a corner of Hauz Shamsi and is believed to date back to the Lodhi era. It was built as a retreat for the emperor in the summer months when the heat and dust of Delhi made life uncomfortable, even for royal families. Or was it a resort for pilgrims? At that time too the capital had many shrines of Muslim saints where people came not only from all over India but also abroad – Afghanistan, Turkey, Iran, Iraq and Arabia to pay homage.

The proverb that a saint of a distant country attracts more admirers held good here too and it was only natural for the ruling dynasty to build pavilions and rest-houses for the pilgrims and their horses or caravans. It was considered not only a work of piety, but also a social obligation and, as a result, the city developed, with more buildings coming up. Not only that, it also created employment for many, though there was no population explosion at that time.

The name Jahaz Mahal is quaint for a palace. Did the name bring solace to foreign pilgrims who arrived by ship and were nostalgic about their own country? Another reason could have been the monarch's love for far away lands and ships, though a journey was denied to him because of State business and also because of the fact that absence from the capital for a long period could lead to somebody seizing power. The ruler in those days was despotic and the king had to show himself every day to his subjects and convince them that he was still in command. Hence the construction of Jahaz Mahal was some consolation for maritime pleasures denied in a landlocked capital where there were lakes and artificial tanks, but no seas – only a river. This of course is only a conjecture considering

The Pankha procession during Phoolwalon-ki-Sair at Jahaz Mahal

the fact that it is not even certain who built Jahaz Mahal, though it is generally conceded that it was constructed after 1451 and before 1526, that is prior to Babar's invasion of India and the advent of Moghul rule. The Lodhi connexion is therefore very much there, for the dynasty did have great builders like Sikandar Lodhi who is said to have founded the city of Agra.

Coming back to Jahaz Mahal one is impressed by its rectangular courtyard in the centre, the arched chambers at the sides and an arch which gives the impression that part of the palace was a mosque. There are blue tiles in the pavilion which leads to the gateway and the monument has square towers or *chhattries* at its corners. It is a romantic building and forms the backdrop of the annual 'Phoolwalon-ki-Sair'.

6

Arabic Sultana's Dream

Apna Utsav has brought back to life many monuments of Delhi. The *shehnai*, the harmonium, the tabla and the sound of anklets reverberate again after centuries of neglect, when the vagabond and the gypsy were their only residents. A bevy of girls in *lehnga* or *gharara* run around the gaunt building that goes by the name of Begampuri Masjid in Begampur village, about 14 km from Delhi city. It lies on the road to Mehrauli. The skirts of the school-girls are colourful. Mirth and song are not allowed in a house of prayer so the girls stay out. You are free to enter the courtyard, provided you observe the usual decorum.

The mosque is one of the seven built during the reign of Firoz Shah Tughlak by his Minister Khan-i-Jehan Junan Shah, a man of deep religious conviction in a despotic age when faith played a big part in the affairs of state and piety had to be displayed like an emblem on a shirtfront. The mosque has a huge courtyard with cloisters at the sides. The corridors have a row of windows and gates on the south, east and north. The main facade of the prayer chamber has in all 34 arched openings and the one in the centre is the most imposing, with two tall minarets at the sides. The chamber is surmounted by a big dome and around it are a number of smaller domes. The whole structure is built of rubble and a fine example of Tughlak architecture.

But if one were to forget one's history for a while, this building might well have been in Samarkand or Badakshan or even in far away Rome, for it seems to have a universal appeal about it. The name Begampuri denotes that it was named after a begum just like the village in which it stands.

The begum could have been of Junan Shah's household – woman pious and faithful who offered prayers five times a day, paid the *zakat* to the needy and observed the month-long fast of *Ramzan* and other tenets of Islam rigidly. A mosque to perpetuate her could be a suitable memorial.

Yet it is not always so. Take the case of the Arabic Sultana who dreamt one night that a torrential stream was emanating from in between her legs in which a multitude of men and women were bathing. The next morning she told her husband about it, and the Caliph summoned all his wise men to interpret the dream. Many tried but failed, and then an old man unravelled the meaning thus: the stream was the Caliph's wealth, and the multitude was the zeal of the faithful waiting to participate in it. Hence the Sultana had to build a canal and a mosque to make her dream come true. She did so and became a religious woman after that.

While you contemplate this story and retrace your steps from the mosque, the air outside is filled with the laughter of the girls and the swish of their skirts. *Apna Utsav* is long over, but thanks to it people have been able to visit old forgotten Begampur.

7

Mosque of the Windows

South of Khirki village in Delhi is a double-storeyed mosque which looks more like a fort than a house of prayer. Built by Junan Shah, *Wazir* of Firoz Shah Tughlak in the 14th century, it has three gateways with imposing minarets that stand out like the fingers of a supplicant pointing towards heaven.

The plastered building gets its name from the Khirkis or perforated windows which have corresponding cells in the first storey. The courtyard has pillars and is covered by nine domes, which is rare for a mosque. Generally this part, where most of the faithful offer prayers, is open to the sky.

Junan Shah built several mosques one of which, similar to Khirki Masjid, is in Nizamuddin. The *Wazir's* zeal for building mosques was not unusual in those days when people welcomed each house of prayer as a propagation of faith and a centre of social welfare, for a *madarsa* or school and rooms for wayfarers were invariably added to it.

Situated on the outskirts of Malviya Nagar, the mosque does not attract many visitiors. Nearby is the village of Khirki which boasts of the tomb of Sheikh Yusuf Qattal, who died in 1527. He was a disciple of Kazi Jallaluddin, a saint of Lahore, and is remembered as a holy man who could work miracles. There are some other graves in the vicinity of the tomb. It is difficult to say who lie buried in them but a safe guess would be that they were people of importance, probably related to the Sheikh Sahib, and venerated after his death. The main tomb rests on 12 pillars and must have been an imposing structure in the medieval days for it still retains traces of grandeur.

Khirki Masjid

But to go back to Khirki Masjid, one wonders why the *Khirkis* were built and for what purpose? Was the mosque meant for the exclusive use of ladies in *purdah*? If so, why is it so large and with so many gateways? Its fort-like structure makes one think that it was sought to be protected, but from what? Was it Mongol invaders? In all probability Khirki Masjid was part of an embattled complex built by Junan Shah for his safety because of the many court intrigues in those days.

From the protected windows of the mosque one could watch happenings outside without fear of getting hit by a traitor's arrow. Such is Khirki Masjid then, a strange mosque in a strange place. It would be worthwhile to renovate it and make it known to tourists and students of architecture for it tells a tale of its own.

8

Lie Here the Sultan

The tomb of Sikandar Lodhi, on the corner of Lodhi Garden, New Delhi, has a gash in its dome, the result of the plaster peeling off, but to a dreamy visitor it is a reminder of the fact that the Sultan's dynasty had suffered a mortal blow. That was in the First Battle of Panipat when Babar defeated his son Ibrahim Lodhi, Sikandar did not live to see that day. After 'life's fitful fever' he sleeps in a place which is quiet and serene.

Nizam Khan Sikandar Lodhi, in whose reign Vasco da Gama landed in India, was the most powerful of the Lodhi rulers.

He made conquests in Bihar and Bengal, subjugated Gwalior and founded the city of Agra in 1504. The story goes that the Sultan set out on horseback from Delhi and rode for three days sleeping in the forest at night and drinking from the wells under the *neem* trees as those over which the tamarind grows are generally not liked.

Sikandar Lodhi and his party passed by Mathura and galloped for several *Kos* before they reined in their horses. Post-lunch the Sultan and his *Wazir* set out in a boat over the Jamuna. When they had sailed for some time, the Sultan asked, "Where shall we found our new city?" The Wazir thought and said, "On this bank." "No," said the Sultan, "that which is agar" (ahead). Thus was the city of Agra founded. But the next year there was a big earthquake in which most of its elegant buildings were destroyed and thousands of people killed."

Ibrahim Lodhi was a child then. He had felt the tremors in Delhi, for the capital also was rocked though the damage here was not so great.

As Ibrahim grew up he became haughty and the power that came into his hands, when Sikandar Lodhi died in 1517, turned him insolent. He would keep his nobles standing for hours to show his contempt for them. Not only they but even his uncle Alam Khan revolted and the Moghuls were able to establish an empire. His father's tomb, therefore, is of special interest to students of history, for had Ibrahim been like him Babar would never have ventured into India.

When you see the octagonal tomb, a typical example of Lodhi architecture, with a covered verandah and symmetrical arches, remember that the man who lies buried in it was a great king but an unfortunate father. Incidentally, Ibrahim Lodhi's tomb is in Panipat, not Delhi.

9

Bahlol Lodhi's Tomb
in Chirag Delhi

The tomb of Bahlol Lodhi is a forgotten monument in Chirag Delhi. It is situated near the shrine of Hazrat Nasiruddin Mahmud (after whom the area is known), for the 14th-century saint is regarded as the 'lamp of Delhi' by his devotees.

It is said that while still young Bahlol and his friends met a dervish who asked each boy by turns if he would like to buy the kingdom of Delhi for 2,000 *tankas*. Only Bahlol agreed and was blessed by the dervish. His friends later made fun of him for being a 'fool'. But Bahlol replied that it was not so, because if the dervish's word was true he stood to gain a kingdom and if it was not so he had done the right thing in giving a *fakir* what he desired.

Bahlol's birth too was unusual. His mother died in a house collapse but he was successfully taken out of her womb and nursed by his aunt and uncle, Sultan Shah Lodhi. Sultan Shah saw signs of greatness in the boy and brought him up accordingly, so much so that he did not even scold him for playing on his *musallah* (prayer mat).

The child grew up into a fine man. At that time Mohammad Shah of the Sayyid dynasty was the ruler of Delhi. But his kingdom was in a mess. Bahlol managed to get himself appointed Governor of Punjab and when Alam Shah succeeded to the throne, he contrived to get the kingdom for himself. One day a group of his followers dressed as *Mirasis* (roadside musicians) tricked the guards into allowing them to enter the house of the powerful *Wazir*, Hamid Khan. They forced him to surrender and after that it was an easy job to oust Alam Shah, though the *khutba* continued to be read in his name.

Alam Shah retired to Badaun and Bahlol became the first ruler of the Lodhi dynasty in 1451. Brave and generous, he was always fond of intellectuals and holy men. Being a good general he conquered Jaunpur, Dholpur and Kalpi. The Sharqis of Jaunpur were the lords of the east and their downfall was the Lodhi's biggest gain.

But Bahlol never let success go to his head. He remained humble, never sitting on a throne but on a carpet along with his nobles. He died in July 1489 after a long reign.

Bahlol's tomb is a drab place compared to other mausoleums. It is a square chamber with three arched openings on all sides, surmounted by five domes, the central one being the biggest. Koranic verses are inscribed on the arches but there is hardly any other ornamentation. Perhaps a tomb which reflects the times in which Bahlol lived – rugged and sans the sophistication of the later rulers. But he was the only one to 'buy' a kingdom from a dervish.

10

Fortress of the Barber

Nai-ka-Kot or barber's fortress, on the outskirts of Delhi proper, is in ruins now and few find the time to visit it for they are not conversant with the history of the place. How could a barber have built a fortress? Barbers were generally poor in the olden days who often did not find much work, for few at that time went about with a clean chin. The hair was usually short-cropped or worn long, reaching right up to the neck, though some preferred to keep it earlong.

There is the tale of a jobless barber who was so henpecked that one day he decided to go into the jungle so that he could fall prey to some wild animal and thus be rid of his earthly woes. But things did not happen the way he had thought they would and, getting scared at nightfall, the poor man climbed a tree. He saw some robbers distributing their booty and shaking with fear fell on them, causing them to run away in confusion. The barber was able to collect all the wealth and live happily ever after.

But this is just a fairy tale and the plight of the barbers was indeed a pitiable one. However, the barbers did occupy a position of some importance in social functions, like marriages and ceremonies associated with child-birth. The royal barber enjoyed a high status because of his closeness to the king. Nai-ka-Kot could be the story of one such barber who was attached to Mohammad bin Tughlak.

The king had a philosophical bent of mind which was compounded by his suspicious nature. The barber who came to trim the royal beard was the source of much news, peppered with rumour and hearsay. Perhaps one day he did manage to hear of a conspiracy and inform the king. In gratitude, Mohammad Tughlak built a fortress to house his informant. But this tale has some loose ends (like the one which says that

The lizard holds its court where emperor and clown once held sway

it was constructed by his *Wazir*) because Nai-ka-Kot is also known as Dhobi (washerman's) Kot and Mehtar Kot (how did a sweeper come to be asociated with this medieval fortress?). Did the king honour a washerman and a sweeper also the way he did the barber? If so, what were the services rendered by the man who washed the royal robes and the one who swept the royal apartments?

Did they also unearth a conspiracy and save the king's life? In the absence of records it is difficult to come to a conclusion.

However, one thing is certain: Nai-ka-Kot was the private apartment of Mohammad bin Tughlak where he retired when he had had enough of the affairs of state. A plausible explanation could be that the barber, the washerman and the sweeper were among the few allowed into the apartment, for without them a fastidious king was unable to lead his personal life in comfort in an age when washing machines and flush toilets were hundreds of years away. And the barber was there to feed the gossip on which Mohammad tested his hairbrained schemes. Courtiers who made fun of the king behind his back probably got a kick out of calling his retreat Nai-ka-Kot and the name stuck for posterity.

11

Bridging Fact and Fiction

Bridges have a tale or two suspended from them. A courtesan danced over the old Jamuna Bridge at Agra in the first decade of the 20th century when Commissioner Martin and his family went for picnics during the monsoon. The dancer must have been a sight against the background of the billowing clouds (*Ghata*) while the picnickers made merry below. The bridges built during the time of Sher Shah and the Moghuls in Delhi had their own yarns. The Bara Pul on the old Mathura Road in the capital was built by Mehr Banu, chief eunuch and chamberlain during the time of Jehangir. It got its name from the 12 piers, each topped by an obelisk. The eunuch built the bridge as an act of piety, for it is believed that those who help travellers find their own sojourn through life less bothersome.

A seven-arched bridge near Sikandar Lodhi's tomb was built during the reign of Akbar by a nobleman. The eight piers and not the arches give it the name of *Athapula*. This bridge spanned a stream that earlier used to claim many lives during the rainy season. The nobleman, Bahadur Khan, nearly got drowned in it himself, but fate was kind and he survived to build the bridge.

The Budhiawallah bridge, constructed during the time of Sher Shah Suri on the old Trunk Road a few miles from Delhi and now within the precincts of an industrial estate on Mathura Road, has an interesting history. It used to be called Sindhu bridge because the road built by Sher Shah led to the Indus. The story goes that during the decadent Moghul period, when law and order had broken down, as there was hardly any authority to enforce it, an old woman decided to make it her observation post.

Budhiawallah bridge

She used to sit on the bridge while below hid her seven sons. The woman would stop each passer-by and ask him for alms. She was smooth-tongued and able to glean enough information to judge whether the person was carrying a lot of money with him. Convinced that it was so she would cry for *pani* (water) in a loud voice. The sons took the hint and robbed the traveller. The unfortunate man was either murdered by them or handed over to their maternal uncles, who were also seven in number and formed the dreaded Mamu gang.

The woman and her sons and brothers were eventually caught and brought to justice. But old wives' tales do not tell us by whom and when. That must have been a long time ago, but the little bridge is still known as Budhiawallah Pul, where many an unwary traveller met his end.

12

Bhuli Bhatyari:
The Fair Inn-keeper

The opening of Bhuli Bhatyari-ka-Mahal to the public is an event of some importance and Delhi Tourism Development Corporation deserves praise for having restored a part of the 650-year-old monument. Built by Firoz Tughlak (1351-1388) it now exists in the form of two gateways and a boundary wall with an open space in between. The wall is about 6 metres high. According to Sir Sayyid Ahmad Khan, the place was once occupied by a nobleman called Bu-Ali Bhati, which in course of time got corrupted to Bhuli Bhatyari.

Most people however believe that Bhuli Bhatyari was some young gram roaster or innkeeper who enjoyed royal patronage. Up to a few years ago *Pavan Parichhana-ka-mela* used to be held at the site to determine the direction of the wind and thereby forecast the prospects for the crops in the coming year. A similar fair was held at Mehrauli where a flag was flown atop the temple of Yogmaya on *Basant Panchami* to predict the agricultural prospects.

Situated on the Ridge, adjacent to Pusa Road, the open ground of the *Mahal* was frequented by *patangbaz* (kite-fliers) because kites were flown there to determine the direction of the wind between *Basant* and *Holi*. Also, *manja*-makers used to make the string for kite-flying nearby. The making of the *manja* is an elaborate process and vast open spaces are needed to wound the thread on stakes driven into the ground, after which it is glazed with a solution containing crushed glass to make it sharp as a knife. The best *manja* is needed for kite tangles and the person who cuts the strings of nine kites one after another gets the title of *Naushera* (or killer of nine tigers).

Bhuli Bhatyari – An artist's conception

Records are silent on how Bhuli Bhatyari-ka-Mahal got reduced to just an open space and two successive gateways. The conjecture is that it was destroyed in an earthquake. There was a very strong earthquake during the reign of Sikandar Lodi, when half the buildings in Agra and many in Delhi collapsed. Some think it was destroyed during the invasion of Taimur which took place in 1399, some 11 years after the death of Firoz Tughlak. But a more fanciful reason was given by Haji Zahoorduddin, who belonged to one of the oldest families of Delhi.

According to the tale heard by him from his grandmother who was born before the 'Mutiny', Bhuli Bhatyari was neither a gram roaster nor an innkeeper but a wayward nymph who appeared to Firoz one afternoon when the emperor had been separated from his entourage during a *shikar* trip and was frantically searching for water. Just when he thought he was going to die of thirst, he saw a young woman carrying a pitcher of water. The emperor called out to her but she did not listen. He followed her on his horse but somehow she managed to keep ahead of him and all his entreaties for a drink of water were ignored.

The girl went round a huge tree and stopped. Firoz dismounted from his horse and thinking that the girl was deaf and dumb conveyed through signs that he was thirsty. The girl smiled and poured water from the pitcher into his cupped hands. The emperor had his fill and when he looked up again he was smitten by love for the girl who was not only beautiful but had also saved his life. He married her but the condition was that he would build a palace for her and visit her either in the afternoon or at night. Soon after his death the palace was destroyed in a mysterious fire. Probably nobody tried to rebuild it and so only the wall and the gateways remain. But if this legend be true how did Bu-Ali Bhatti get to occupy the *Mahal*?

13

Well Among Skyscrapers

Raja Ugrasen was the legendary founder of the Agarwal community in the dim past and like Raja Bhoj, his must have been a court of splendour where the animals too got the justice they deserved, a kingdom where the lion and the lamb drank at the same point in the stream. The *baoli* or step-well said to have been built by Ugrasen in Delhi, is hidden behind huge buildings now and one can approach it via Hailey Road which commemorates the great Anglo-Indian, Sir Malcolm Hailey a friend of Nawab Mohammad Faiyaz Khan of Agra, a city with which Ugrasen's name is closely associated. There are thick walls all around the well which give the impression that they were built in the Tughlak period when this kind of architecture was in vogue. The *baoli* is about 15 metres wide and 60 metres in length with steps leading right down to the water level.

With the approach of summer, the *baoli* begins to attract people who go there for swimming or to escape the heat of the afternoon, for it is as cool as a *hammam*; the thick rubble walls helping to keep out the sun's strong rays. Like many ancient monuments, this one too was built upon by the Sultans of the medieval period and improved. It must have lain neglected for centuries in an age when New Delhi was not even a remote possibility, for most of what constitutes this area now was a jungle which only *shikaris* frequented to hunt for blue-bull, deer and partridge. It was they who made use of the *baoli* to quench their thirst after a long chase or for a bath to wash off the dust and the heat.

Those who haunt the *baoli* now are not *shikaris* but people denied the cool comfort of air-conditioners and electric fans. Among them are some vagabonds too, though it must be conceded that poverty makes one look a suspect in the eyes of the well-to-do. What draws them to the baoli is the

Ugrasen's *baoli*

common bond that binds the poor, and they have the knack of finding their own amusements. Spend an afternoon with them and you will come back wiser.

The young and the healthy dive into the waters of the *baoli* from atop the massive walls, and most of them wear the 'langot' in preference to swimming trunks, which are meant for more sophisticated resorts. As a little form throws itself into the water with a loud splash the men playing *pacchisi* (Indian ludo) heave a collective sigh as it disturbs their concentration, but have to pass the time all the same. There are others besides them who come to gossip or to tell yarns, which are as old as Raja Bhoj.

Others talk about the exploits of Raja Ugrasen and of the need for him to build the *baoli* that still bears his name. Why did he build it? History books may be silent, but gossip-mongers know more. It was a gift for a beautiful *rani* who liked to dwell in a thicket. Some say she was not really a princess, but a fairy. Whatever it was, Ugrasen did a wise thing in building the *baoli*, for people even now bless him for it. That some misuse it for anti-social activities or for commiting suicide was not his fault.

MOGHUL ERA

14

Khan-e-Khanan's Tomb

The mausoleum of Abdul Rahim Khan-e-Khanan in Nizamuddin does not glitter on moonlit nights because it is made of red sandstone and not of marble like the Taj. Yet, the discerners find in its design a similarity with the Taj, and that is no wonder for it is an example of Moghul architecture in its heyday. This despite the fact that the building has been shorn of its splendour, with its ornamental slabs having been removed to beautify Safdarjang's Tomb and Asif-ud-Daulah's creations in Lucknow. As a matter of fact, this 360-year-old tomb gives the impression of having been pecked at by some giant bird out to despoil the last resting place of a great nobleman, soldier, poet and scholar whose contribution was akin to that of the celebrated Amir Khusrau.

Abdul Rahim was the son of the great Bairam Khan, Akbar's kinsman and guide and the friend of Humayun, with whom he escaped to Persia after Sher Shah had temporarily ended Moghul rule in India. Bairam Khan was one of those hardy and trusted generals who helped Babar in his many conquests until that worthy had established himself on the throne of Delhi. So strong was Bairam Khan that when an elephant ran amok he jumped down from the balcony of his palace with a sword in his mouth and cut off its trunk before the infuriated animal could trample down a young woman and her child. The confidant of three of the greatest Moghul emperors could not but father a son like Abdul Rahim.

After the assassination of Bairam Khan at the hands of an Afghan whose father had been put to death on his orders, Akbar took the young Abdul Rahim under his care. The youth flourished and such were his achievements that the great Moghul invested him with the title of Khan-e-Khanan or the Khan of Khans. Abdul Rahim not only distinguished

The mausoleum of Khan-e-Khanan

himself on the battlefield, but also in the field of letters. Seeing his accomplishments the emperor appointed him tutor to Prince Salim. But when the latter became emperor he removed the Khan-e-Khanan from his high office at the instigation of Nur Jehan. He died at Lahore and his body was brought to Delhi to be buried in the mausoleum he had erected in his life-time. It stares one in the face like an enigma now.

Abdul Rahim Khan-e-Khanan was a master of several languages, including Persian, Hindi and Sanskrit. His 'dohas', famous as 'Rahim ke dohe', rank with those of Kabir and one need not be a poet to understand their relevance even in our own prosaic times.

15

Here Rest the Moghuls

Where do most of the Moghul kings, princes and princesses sleep in Delhi? The answer is not on beds of asphodel but in the vaults of Humayun's Tomb, built with much devotion, by the emperor's first wife, Haji Begum. Among the well-known ones buried here are Hamida Bano Begum, the mother of Akbar the Great, Dara Shikoh, Shah Jehan's heir apparent, Aurangzeb's once beloved son, Azam Shah, the dandy Jahandar Shah, and his slayer Farrukhseyar, Ahmed Shah and Alamgir-II. There are many more of lesser name and fame, some without inscriptions too, though not confined to the dustbin of history, but gathered within the folds of the mausoleum of their cherished ancestor Humayun. One gets the strange feeling of beds spread on a summer night with the kind emperor sleeping in glory among many of those who waded to the throne through the blood of their relatives. The last rites of the murdered princes were generally adhered to and they were laid to rest in the family graveyard. But there were exceptions like Dara Shikoh, who was denied even the ritual funeral bath by his austere brother Aurangzeb.

In Mehrauli the precincts of the shrine of Hazrat Qutubuddin Bakhtiar Kaki also form the burial ground of many Moghul and other princes. In Agra, Akbar's tomb at Sikandra is the repository of the remains of a host of princes and princesses. In Calcutta, several descendants of Wajid Ali Shah, the last king of Oudh, lie buried, and in Rangoon, the family of Bahadur Shah Zafar has found a burial place denied to it in the land of its birth.

Actually, Babar's tomb should have been the last resting place of all those descendants whose graves are found in Humayun's mausoleum. But Babar chose to be buried in far-away Kabul which ceased to be a part of the

Moghul empire by the time most not-so-distinguished of his successors died. Had Babar's body not been taken away from the Aram Bagh the funeral vaults of the house of Taimur would probably have been located in Agra and not in Nizamuddin area of Delhi. Isn't it an irony of fate that the first and last emperors could not be buried in India? While Babar loved Kabul, Bahadur Shah Zafar had no choice as the British wanted to stamp out his very memory by burying him in a nondescript grave in Rangoon, which was redisovered by chance and formed the rallying point for Netaji Subhas Chandra Bose's INA during World War-II.

The *mazar* has now become a place of pilgrimage in Myanmar, where the last emperor is worshipped as a *Pir*. Babar's mausoleum is however a modest one, which lay neglected for many years. But it is heartening to note that lately it has been renovated, having somehow escaped destruction during the Soviet occupation of Afghanistan and then the turmoil of the Taliban period. Though demands have been made for bringing back Zafar's remains to India, nobody has raised his voice for Babar's reburial, not entirely because of the first Moghul emperor's dying wish.

So Humayun's Tomb remains the funeral parlour of the family of Babar. You go from vault to vault and nothing but stones confront you, the tombstones of history, so to say, in each of which is enshrined a cloak-and-dagger mystery, and death, gruesome death, generally at the hands of an assassin hired by the next of kin, the ambitious prince determined to seize the throne by the foulest means. Many of them were done to death by their brothers, uncles, nephews, cousins or treacherous *Wazirs*.

Some died of poison, administered through a favourite, but faithless, courtesan, others strangled in their sleep, yet others hacked with the sword or stabbed through the heart or back. Little children too were not spared. Who knows they may have made better kings than those who engineered their murder. There might have been some among them who might have excelled Akbar; Dara surely for he was the prince of princes.

You gaze at these tombstones with awe and pity. How many innocent lives destroyed for the sake of ambition! It seems as though the Angel of Destruction holds court in the vaults of Humayun's Tomb. There is the silence of death all around, with the Grim Reaper gloating over his sickle of time with which he has laid low both those with name and those without fame. Only Clio understands the secrets of these vaults and it is she who weeps in them through her tresses:

Put on your shoes and tip-toe away lest you disturb the eternal sleep of the royal house of Taimur.

16

Moghul Treasure

Where has all the treasure of the Moghuls gone? There is no trace of it. But if you believe an old man, all that vast collection of gold, silver and precious stones was not looted, nor usurped by the British but pawned to the bullion dealers of Agra, Delhi, Lahore and Jaipur. At least a substantial part of it by the pauper Moghul kings and princes who were nevertheless great believers in the power bestowed by precious stones.

The old man sits on the pavement in Nabi Karim, Delhi, with a glass case in which are rings, pendants, brooches, necklaces and 'precious stones'. He hardly seems to get any customers, and the few that come out of curiosity go away with the proverbial flea in the ear.

The man talks of precious stones as though they were genie entrapped by him for the well-being of his clients. You tell him your zodiac sign and he will recommend the stone that will suit you best.

If your sign is Aries it's a ruby for you, for Taurus it's turquoise, for Gemini a topaz, for Cancer a pearl, for Leo a diamond, for Virgo an agate, for Libra a sapphire, for Scorpio a bloodstone, for Sagittarius an amethyst, for Capricorn a garnet, for Aquarius an opal, and for Pisces an emerald.

The diamond is a coloured or tinted brilliant stone of pure carbon; the colour of the ruby varies from deep crimson or purple to pale rose; the turquoise is opaque, skyblue or greenish blue; the topaz is transparent, yellow, white, green, blue or colourless; the pearl is white or bluish - grey with a beautiful lustre; the agate is hard banded chalcedony; the bloodstone is green chalcedony spotted or striped with red; the amethyst is purple or violet; the garnet transparent deep red; the opal milk-white or bluish with green yellow and red reflections; the emerald is bright green; and the sapphire transparent blue.

The old man describes the colours of each stone and their properties. Now Aries represents the ram and the ruby is linked with it for protection and prosperity; Taurus, the bull, is calmed by the turquoise stone. The Gemini twins or *Ashwini Kumars* love the topaz. Cancer, the crab, prefers the pearl for it is not satisfied with anything less.

Leo, the lion, likes the hard diamond, which is as tough as it. Virgo, the virgin or *Kanya*, merges with the agate. Libra or scales balances with the sapphire. Scorpio, the eternal scorpion, has its sting tied to the bloodstone. Sagittarius, the archer, will have nothing but the amethyst. Capricorn, the goat, chews the 'sweet curd' of garnet. Aquarius, the water-carrier, loves the opal; and Pisces or fishes like to swim with the emerald.

What happens if a Capricornian wears an amethyst? The old man shakes his forefinger.

> He will lose his sense of judgement. An Aquarian may meet with an accident if he wears a bloodstone, a Leo would go soft in the head if his ring has an agate, a Geminian may become a pauper for sporting a ruby, and a Sagittarian will fall from grace if he wears an emerald just as a Libran will become restless if he spurns the sapphire.

One wonders at the words of the old man and his strong belief that imparts the halo of the zodiac to the pavement. Now the zodiac is the heavenly belt that includes all positions of the sun, the moon and the planets as known to the ancients and divided into 12 parts. The zodiacal light is the luminous triangular area of the sky seen at sunrise in the east and at sunset in the west.

How do precious stones influence the zodiac? You may believe in it or not and instead of buying a ruby or an agate just acquire a plain ring or a brooch, the old man is not bothered. He only bargains for the stones and that too when he is satisfied that they will suit your sign. To support his belief he quotes the Moghuls.

If one goes to Dariba Kalan in Chandni Chowk one can be assured of getting genuine stones, not the imitation ones sold on the pavement. Some of the jewellers have been in business since the time of Shah Alam in whose grandsire's reign Nadir Shah invaded Delhi and took away enormous booty.

The throne upon which the Moghul emperors sat – the famous Peacock Throne was estimated to have cost six million sterling – and the palace was worthy of the throne.

Joannes de Laet, the Flemish geographer, philologist and naturalist, was a director of the Dutch East India Company, which established a factory at Agra in 1621 with Francisco Pelsaert at its head.

A contribution considered important to history, says 'Thomas Smith', is made by de Laet in his book on the Moghul empire. Speaking of the treasures of Akbar and Jehangir in the fort of Agra, he states:

> On the death of Akbar, grandfather of the prince now reigning (Shah Jahan), his treasures were carefully counted and were found to amount in all, including gold, silver and copper wrought and unwrought, together with jewels and all manner of household commodities to 34 crores, 82 laks and 26,386 rupees. Of the total Rs. 198,346,6663/4 was specie of all descriptions.

This treasure, he said, included 24,000 beautifully bound books written by great authors and valued at Rs. 6,463,731 of that time. This was certainly as precious a part of the great treasure – it was accumulated since the time of Akbar the Great.

The treasure in Agra Fort was estimated at 20 million pounds and that in the six sub-treasuries in the fortresses of Gwalior, Narwar, Ranthambhor, Asirgarh, Rohtas and Lahore (the biggest of the six) also at 20 million.

Akbar also owned 6,751 elephants, 12,000 horses, 6,223 camels and dromedaries and 7,260 mules and oxen.

Jehangir's famous chain of justice, which was thirty yards long and had sixty bells on it, was made of pure gold and weighed six *maunds*. The daily outlay at the court of Agra came to Rs. 50,000, including sums spent in feeding the elephants and other beasts and on the royal food and dress, etc. at a time when the buying power of money was 500 times of what it is now.

The Moghul treasures increased considerably during the reigns of Jehangir and Shah Jahan. The latter, had a store of 3,000 million rupees while King Henry VII, who died in 1509, left 1,800,000 in bullion and was considered rich.

Although the fabulous wealth has gone its way, the bullion merchants are still rich. Not so the old man of Nabi Karim who sells imitation stones and dreams of real ones which belonged to the Moghuls.

17

A 'Babari' Mosque

Palam village is a relic of Dhilli or Dhillika, founded by the Tomars, which later came to be known as Dilli or Delhi. The ancient name of Palam is Palamba and some historians trace its antiquity to Raja Soni, the founder of Sonepat, who was the 13th in descent from Arjuna. The village was flourishing at the time of Mohammad bin Tughlak, in whose reign the Moorish traveller Ibn Batuta visited it.

He was a native of Tangiers who came to India in 1333 and remained in Delhi until 1342 after being appointed Chief *Qazi*. Batuta described Delhi as "a most magnificent city, its mosques and walls without an equal on earth." But he observed that although the king was then repeopling it (after his futile experiment to transfer the capital to Daulatabad), it was almost a desert. "The greatest city in the world has the fewest inhabitants", he said. What a contrast to present-day Delhi, almost bursting at the seams, and extending even to the remotest pockets which were once thinly populated villages!

One of the landmarks of Palam village (besides the airport to which it has given its name) is the mosque said to have been constructed by a nobleman called Ghaznafar in about AD 1528, which makes it perhaps the only structure of Babar's reign in Delhi that has survived the ravages of time. The mosque is built of *Kakaia eent* (small bricks), with three arched openings leading to its not very large prayer chamber. On the four corners of the roof are small minarets with domes. There are Persian and Arabic inscriptions on the mosque which give the date of its construction as 935 AH (Al Hijri).

One is inclined to believe that either this mosque was rebuilt by the illustrious Ghaznafar or there was another masjid in the village that naturally called for an inspection by the Chief Qazi (Ibn Batuta). The Moor's *Travelogue*, written after his return to Tangiers, is about the most truthful account of the reign of Mohammad Tughlak. Batuta was a keen observer, who would have made a fine journalist in more recent times, and little seems to have escaped his eye.

Palam was also famous for its *baoli* or step-well, with a Sanskrit incription, believed to have been written in 1276 during the reign of Balban, one of the great Slave rulers. This means that Palam was more than a village in those times.

Even as late as the time of Shehzada Ali Gohar, who ruled as Shah Alam II from 1759 to 1806, Palam was considered an important suburb of the capital. As a matter of fact, the popular saying then was "Az Dilli ta Palam Badshah Shah Alam", a poignant assessment of the domain of the blind emperor (Andha Moghul to the residents of old Palam).

18

Mysterious Forbidden Gate

The Purana Qila in Delhi never ceases to confound the visitor. Take its northern gate which is known as the Talaqi Darwaza. Some say it means Forbidden Gate; others think it is the gate of special entry. Built by Sher Shah Suri it has a panel showing a man fighting a lion which is considered unusual in a Moghul era monument. Perhaps the panel commemorates the fight Sher Shah had when as a young man he killed a 'Sher'. Since then Farid Khan came to be known as Sher Afghan.

But why was this scene carved on the Forbidden Gate? It was Humayun who built his capital Dinpanah here over the ruins of an old fort, below which lay the legendary city of Indraprastha. When Sher Shah ousted Humayun and built his own fort he probably retained the gate marked 'Forbidden' by Humayun; forbidden because only the emperor, his children and the ladies of the harem could enter or leave through this gate.

Another reason could be that it led to the heritage of the Pandavas, with its haunted palaces and 'Magic Casements' opening, not to 'Perilous Seas' but to the swift currents of the Jamuna which flowed so close by that it filled the moat.

Humayun and Sher Shah were not iconoclasts like Mahmud of Ghazni. They were enlightened emperors who had great curiosity about the past. Could it be that they were carrying on excavations of their own and discovering the mysteries of the Mahabharat era? The Forbidden Gate hence barred entry to all and sundry and was open only to the chosen few.

The marble panels are more than the tale of Sher Shah and his fight with the king of beasts. Such depictions were a common feature in ancient Babylon. The lion, besides man, is among the four living creatures (one 'full of eyes in front and behind') that are believed to surround the highest seat of heaven. This is part of the Semitic story of creation and the panel of the Talaqi Darwaza may well have been inspired by it, for Sher Shah killed a tiger, not a lion.

Even so when the Purana Qila is lit up at night you 'see' the ghosts of history parading themselves in all their splendour. Drive past it and feel the impact of the centuries. The Kurus, Guptas, Arabs, Pathans, Moghuls and many more held sway there. The crumbling walls say as much. They have been built and rebuilt, the trees that grow near them perhaps germinated from earlier ones and so the place has preserved an atmosphere that defies time and age.

Lingering before those hallowed walls one could see the stones and crevices highlighted by the strong lights that illuminate them. An owl flew in circles till it found a perch on the ruined citadel of mighty empires which once drew awe and wonder because of the superpowers who ruled them. The Indraprastha of the Pandavas flourished there with its fairy castles and magic fountains. Came the successors of the mighty Kurus and then invaders. The fort was at a vantage-point and they built on it according to their needs.

Night imparts its own strange hues to buildings old and new. At the Purana Qila it seems to merge with hoary time and you begin to hear the sound of trumpets, the battle-cry of the warriors, the clash of swords, the whiz of a thousand arrows, the neighing of horses, the thunderous trumpeting of elephants and the piteous moans of the fallen being trampled upon by man and beast. This last especially unnerves you, for surely countless people died under these walls in more gruesome ways than you can imagine.

A hare scurries across the road and finds refuge in the many shrubs growing below the ruined walls. It certainly hasn't escaped from the nearby zoo. Suddenly a tiger roars (or is it a lion?), probably finding the mosquitoes too much of a nuisance in its enclosure. The roar sends shivers down the spine, perhaps some subconscious fear from the time when our ancestors faced the king of the jungle – or was it so, for it was all jungle in the primeval past – in an effort to establish their supremacy?

No one utters a word, and yet you feel and hear so much just by watching this deserted monument floodlit. Light and shadow makes all the difference; added to it is the silence of the night. One of those moments when the heavy traffic is absent.

Here history is unfolded before the eyes. You see emperor and clown for what they really were and you hear the perennial song of humanity – of wars and conflicts, peace and tranquillity, the power and glory and then neglect and decay. Is the owl sitting on the wall brooding over the past? Who knows it may be true ! You shrug your shoulders and soon the car leaves such fancies far behind.

19

Milestones

Few visitors to the Delhi zoo perhaps notice a nondescript obelisk in a corner which stands as a mute sentinel of former times. The obelisk is not the only one of its kind. As a matter of fact, there in a whole row of them dotting the road from Delhi to Agra, right up to the Red Stonehorse near Sikandra, where rests Akbar the Great. These (Kos Minars) obelisks do not commemorate any historical event, like they do in Egypt. They are merely reminders of milestones in the Moghul days (although Sher Shah Suri erected some too) when the horse was the fastest mode of conveyance. In fact, it is recorded that Akbar once reached Gujarat in 11 days on horseback from his capital at Fatehpur Sikri to rout his half-brother and other relatives who were trying to usurp power. Roused from sleep the young rebels rubbed their eyes in disbelief, saying:

> But 11 days ago our spies brought word that the emperor was making merry in the company of his courtiers and the women of the harem. How then can he be here in person so soon?

Taken by surprise thus, they fled in disarray. Was this a tribute to Akbar's horsemanship or to the good condition of the roads in his empire? Perhaps to both or else the rebellion would not have ended so soon.

But surprisingly enough the obelisks on the Delhi-Agra Road seem to be among the few preserved in this part of the country though you will find some more up north right up to Lahore. It was at these milestones that the emperor, his messengers or generals changed horses. A man sitting on top of the obelisk spotted the travellers a mile away and the drummer nearby started beating a drum to warn the *sawars* at the next obelisk to keep fresh horses ready for the oncoming party. This way the Moghuls, it

A Moghul milestone

is said, covered the distance from Delhi to Agra in a day. Of course, there were times when the royal party was composed of carts in which travelled the *purdah* ladies and the women who entertained the emperor and his entourage. They reached their destination in about a week's time, with pleasure pavilions springing on the roadside and the nautch girls making the evening sweet and gay.

The obelisk in the zoo has probably got isolated because the road to Agra does not run the same way as it used to in olden days. As such one wonders if this obelisk was the first milestone and whether some of the debauch kings of later times made all the more merry here at the start or end of a journey? Whatever it is, no slender limbs of a dancer embrace the obelisk now; only the flowers of the zoological garden provide it with the tender touch of bygone times.

20

Ghalib's Tomb:
The Muse's Bower

Where Ghalib rests the Muse seems to linger. But one has the feeling that he couldn't be resting peacefully in Nizamuddin, for he was essentially a man of the walled city of Delhi whose charms began and ended within its confines.

The charms are still reflected in a slight difference in speech, the flavour of the *kababs* and the taste of the water from Hare-Bhare Sahib. The breeze that springs from the Jamuna goes past the Red Fort, negotiates the many lanes of the Jama Masjid area and merges with the smell of the *motia* and *chameli* sold at the cross-roads before cooling the courtyards of the houses in the narrow gullies.

Ghalib liked to move about in this area of which the Kashmiri and Delhi gates were the two extremities, with the fort being the hub and centre and the mosque the cultural bastion of the city. Yes, of course, Ghalib always had a soft corner for Agra, because he was born there and passed his boyhood in Kala Mahal from which the Taj looks just like a building in the next locality.

But his heart had been won over by Shahjahanabad. From Ballimaran to Jama Masjid the walk was long enough via Chandni Chowk. Sometimes one could meet Mir Ashiq who came from the opposite direction and went back to his *kucha* via Ballimaran. Was the tilt of his cap different from that of the residents of Nizamuddin? People noticed such traits and developed their pet notions.

Incidentally, it is said of Mir Ashiq that he came armed with a sword and a kafan (burial cloth) tied to his head to save a commoner from a

Ghalib's Tomb in Nizamuddin

band of badmashas just because the poor man used to salam him while he was on his evening walk.

For a man of such intense likes and dislikes as Ghalib, his grave in Nizamuddin is out of the milieu in which he flourished. It's a small enclosure though beautiful in its own way where sparrows make love in the afternoon. The illiterate take it for another shrine where obeisance must be paid, and budding poets hope to imbibe some of the virtues of the great 'shair'.

An old man who sometimes steals up to the mausoleum feels that even a blank page touching the 'mazar' would instantly be graced with a *ghazal*. He has never seen it happen, nor would we surely, but such feelings are the stuff legends are made of.

21

Oudh's Link with Delhi

The last vestige of Moghul architecture exists on the road to the Qutb, which one revisited recently under overcast skies. It is Safdarjang's Tomb and commemorates Mansoor Ali Khan Safdarjang, the second *Nawab* of Oudh. Designed on the pattern of Humayun's Tomb, it is a poor imitation and does not stand comparison with the older building on the aesthetic and architectural levels. The three-storey tomb in fawn-coloured stone also bears a faint resemblance to Akbar's mausoleum at Sikandra, but lacks the magnificence of the latter. Even so it is an interesting monument, situated amidst a garden of 300 square yards, and enclosed by a wall at the corners of which stand octagonal towers.

Arcaded pavilions, named Moti Mahal, Badshah Pasand and Jangli Mahal, have been constructed on the northern, southern and eastern sides, like the pavilions in the outer quadrangle of the Taj. It is believed that these were meant for the accommodation of nobles who visited the mausoleum and could not return home quickly because journeys took so long in the days of animal-driven carriages and travellers had perforce to camp for days on reaching their destination.

The tomb has a carved cenotaph in the central chamber within which is another chamber containing two unmarked graves, both with earthen mounds above them. In it lie buried Mirza Muquim Abul Mansoor Khan Safdarjang, and his wife Banu Begum. The monument was built by their son Shujauddaulah at a cost of Rs. 3 lakhs with a lot of marble and other material being pinched from the mausoleum of the Khan-e-Khanan and other Moghul buildings to embellish the tomb.

Safdarjang was the *Wazir* of Oudh at the court of Mohammad Shah and later the head of the Shia Irani Party and Prime Minister at the court of Ahmed Shah (1748-1754). His opponents were the leaders of the Sunni Turani party headed by Imtiaz-uddaulah and Imadad-ul-Mulk, grandson of the famous Nizam-ul-Mulk. Safdarjang was dismissed because of his failures as Prime Minister and retired to Lucknow where he succeeded his uncle to the throne of Oudh. He died at Faizabad in 1754 and his body was brought for burial to Delhi, for though he had to leave the Moghul court in disgrace he nevertheless pined for his days of grandeur in the Capital and desired that he be laid to rest there.

Looking at the floodlit tomb now one is reminded of the nobleman and his life and times. His mausoleum is as haphazard as his own life was, with Moghul, Rajput, Iranian and Egyptian architecture jostling for space in the building. Incidentally, his son, Shujauddaulah, who was reputed to have the biggest moustaches in the whole Moghul empire, rose to greater eminence, and as the *Wazir* of Shah Alam won back the position his father had lost to the Sunni Party.

In 1761 the *Wazir* played a big role, along with the *Nawab* of Bengal, to contain the power of the British and perpetuate the Moghul dynasty. But the scheme failed when Shah Alam and his supporters were defeated at the Battle of Buxar (1764). It was then that the English were granted the *Diwani* of Bengal after which they had the emperor in their clutches.

Safdarjang's Tomb reminds us of all this and also of the handsome eunuch whom he proclaimed as *Padshah* after his dismissal by Ahmed Shah, declaring him to be the grandson of Kambaksh, the youngest son of Aurangzeb. But that ploy was just as flimsy as his tomb which has been aptly termed as "the last flickering lamp of Moghul architecture".

22

Robert Clive's Pensioner

Looking at Najaf Khan's massive tomb opposite Safdarjang airport one is transported to the times of Nadir Shah, the Persian with piercing eyes who lay waste Delhi during the reign of Mohammad Shah. Najaf Khan was Nadir's victim not in India but in Persia itself, for he belonged to the Safvi dynasty of Iran which was persecuted by the usurper. Najaf and his sister were both jailed, but their plight moved Mohammad Shah, who sent his emissary Mirza Mohsin, to effect the release of the two on compassionate grounds.

Perhaps Nadir's compassion was leavened by the fact that he had already drained the Moghul treasury and carried away its priceless jewels along with the wealth of Delhi and other Indian cities.

By exchanging turbans with Mohammad Shah he had come in possession of the 'Kohinoor' and by right of conquest he had walked away with the 'Peacock Throne'. So setting Najaf and his sister free at the request of his former adversary was a compensation of sorts.

Najaf, only 13 then, accompanied Mohsin, who had married his sister in a case of love at first sight, to India and grew up into a brave young man. His exploits in Bengal were such that even the English generals of the East India Company sought his services. Najaf served them well and was rewarded with an annual pension of Rs. 2 lakhs by no less a person than Robert Clive. But this amount was to be paid from the pension granted to Shah Alam; so naturally Najaf attached himself to the emperor and when the latter moved to Delhi after the Treaty of Allahabad, he became the *Wazir* at the Moghul court.

Nawab Najaf Khan was an orthodox man who never drank or indulged in the passions of the flesh. He was a stern soldier and a clever courtier with a spy system that kept him informed of the goings-on inside the homes of every nobleman of worth. If so and so *begum* refused to kiss her elderly husband on her wedding night, Najaf Khan was duly informed so that he could make use of this knowledge if the need arose.

But power corrupts and Najaf slowly became as debauched as any other nobleman of his time, fleeting away his time in the *zenana* amidst wine, women and song. He died in 1782 a wreck of a man and was buried in the mausoleum he had planned for himself. The monument now is approached through a domeless and pillarless expanse of a compound leading to a barren platform and vaulted chambers containing the graves of Najaf Khan and his daughter, Fatima.

It is a monument that transports one to the Middle East of Ozymandias, though the name of its builder is kept alive on thousands of tongues which prattle on the Najafgarh drain that assumes such importance during the monsoon. And in distant Powys, Wales, Robort Clive's descendant, the present Lord Clive, still chuckles when he hears Najaf Khan's name while strolling among the white peacocks – the progeny of the ones his ancestor took away from India – along with inmense wealth of the Moghuls and their Satraps.

23

Lal Bangla of Lal Kanwar?

Lal Bangla, a landmark of the Delhi Golf Club, has undergone repairs and one is tempted to relate the story of the vivacious Lal Kanwar, the courtesan supposed to be buried there. Jahandar Shah's concubine, as she is known in history, held centre stage in Delhi, Agra and Lahore during the one-year rule of that frivolous emperor in 1712. He ascended the throne after a battle of succession following the death of Bahadur Shah I, Aurangzeb's son and successor.

Lal Kanwar was the daughter of Khasuriat Khan, a descendant of Mian Tansen, and captivated Jahandar Shah, who was more than double her age, by her wit, charm, coquettishness and skill in dancing and singing. As a matter of fact, her actions were compared to those of a nimble fairy and her voice to that of the *houris* of paradise. Her family was one of singers, drummers and fiddlers (*Kalawant*) and earned its livelihood as such.

It is said that when Jahandar Shah first heard her sing, he got so charmed by her voice that he carried her in his arms to an inside room. There undressing Lal Kanwar he asked her to sing again and then made love to her, staying on till the wee hours, for he was convinced that he had found a *mehbooba* (beloved) at last.

The infatuation grew and eventually Lal Kanwar was brought to the Red Fort. She was given the exalted title of 'Imtiaz Mahal' and her brother Niamat Khan Kalawant appointed Governer of Multan. The appointment was cancelled when the *Wazir* asked him to supply 1,000 sarangis in lieu of the governorship and he could not comply with the demand. There is much more than this to the story for the *Wazir's* action made the emperor realize his folly.

In Delhi Lal Kanwar made merry in the fort, making the emperor respond to her whims. They would go out incognito to worship at the various shrines and bathe at the tank attached to the *mazar* of Hazrat Nasiruddin Chirag Delhi, thinking that thus they would draw the blessing of the saint for the birth of a son and heir.

At Lahore the two held festivals of light thrice a month, resulting in a big increase in the price of oil, so much so that even scholars of Persian thought it worthwhile to sell oil and reap a windfall (*Parhein Farsi bechen tel/Yah dekho qudrat ke khel*). The saying couldn't have applied more aptly. At Lahore the emperor had to flee from the battlefield and Lal Kanwar found shelter in what was once the palace of Dara Shikoh.

After losing another battle at Agra, Jahandar Shah and Lal Kanwar escaped in a bullock cart, begging their meals all the way to Delhi and nobody recognized them for they were almost in rags. Many took them for roadside performers, and at Mathura an attempt was made by a gang of ruffians to carry away Lal Kanwar, but smooth-tongued and witty as she was, the ex-dancing girl was able to fool them and make good her escape. The story goes that one of the gangsters tried to pinch her and she cried out so loud, holding her hip, that the others fell on their comrade and started beating him, while Lal Kanwar managed to sneak into the darkness and join her royal lover who was hiding in a tree.

Their follies and foibles were cut short in Delhi when Farrukhseyar overthrew Jahandar Shah with the help of the Sayyid brothers and imprisoned his uncle in Salimgarh, where Lal Kanwar also joined him. Here the ousted emperor was murdered and his consort forced to pass her days in the widows' quarters of the Red Fort. Jahandar Shah was buried in a vault in Humayun's Tomb but it is not known how and why an imposing memorial was built for Lal Kanwar, and by whom?

Most of the juicy stories about her love life were passed on to posterity by Donna Juliana, a Portuguese lady. That she was beautiful and much sought after by men before her romance with Jahandar Shah is beyond doubt. Also beyond doubt is her love for the clownish emperor who doted on her till his dying day, vowing that no bathroom used by Lal Kanwar could stink. Such was the extent of his infatuation, which rivalled that of the celebrated Majnu, who saw the horned moon in the lavatory basin on which Laila squatted.

Standing before the Lal Bangla who can imagine that it is the mausoleum of a courtesan who rose to become empress of India? It was only for a few months that the swish of Begum Imtiaz Mahal's *gharara* turned many heads in the Red Fort where the Rang Mahal was the focus of merry-making every evening. It is a far cry from there to the Lal Bangla, you will agree. However, it is said Shah Alam's mother is also buried there. She too was named Lal Kanwar. In that case the monument commemorates two women, the older one sharing her last abode with a far more respectable personage, for whom perhaps the imposing edifice was later erected to enclose the already existing grave of the senior Lal Kanwar. Historians, however, have their doubts and a few even think she found a lowly grave in some forsaken area and that Shah Alam's sister is the other person buried in the Lal Bangla.

24

The Swings of Sawan

The swings of *Sawan* have always exercised a pull on the imagination and form the theme of our best folk songs. In Mathura and Vrindavan people have been singing these songs for 3,000 years now, ever since Krishna-lore began.

Swings in the Indian ambience were something peculiar to the invaders who came from time to time. Alexander the Great and Chingez Khan might not have found the time to appreciate them but they attracted many rulers all right and also Amir Khusrau later, who served seven Sultans and wrote many of the ditties which women still hum to this day.

Later, the Moghuls became enamoured of them. Some of the swings set up in the Agra Fort were carried away to Deeg by Raja Suraj Mal Jat. Incidentally, they boast of a *Sawan-Bhadon* there too, though the more famous pavilion to perpetuate the rainy months was built in the Red Fort, where mangoes were cooled and eaten to the accompaniment of the *malhar* amid the roll of thunder and lightning flashes. It was in the Baradari built in the middle of the pavilion that the *dilbar* (beloved) came in the form of the Urdu Muse to Bahadur Shah Zafar and did not leave him till his death.

The Indian summer, so detested by Babar, who found an escape from it in the *hammams* and pleasure gardens, was endured by Humayun and liked by Akbar because of the rains that followed. Jehangir was a lover of the meadows of Kashmir but Shah Jehan created his own pleasure domes wherever he stayed. Aurangzeb, a soldier-king, was indifferent to such charms and those who served him had little choice but to stay put in Delhi and seek their attractions in it or in the Deccan.

The swings of the Moghuls were modelled on those of the Rajput rulers and graced the open spaces of the Agra Fort, Fatehpur Sikri and

Sawan-Bhadon pavilion in the Red Fort

later the Red Fort. But the largest number were to be found in Mehrauli, where the latter Moghuls spent the rainy season.

Baghon mein par gaaye hain jhoole, sang the poet and the court of Akbar Shah II moved to Mehrauli. His son Zafar followed him to these delights. The swings in Mehrauli were the ordinary rope ones and the tallest trees were picked for them. One swung in a mango grove and went so high sometimes as to pluck a mango and pass it on to the object of one's desire, for isn't 'aam' the fruit of sensual delight?

Women naturally were on the swing most of the time. Maids pulled the ropes for the princesses, though at times the roles were reversed. However, men too were fond of swinging. One remembers the story of the prince who was given a *Unani* drug by a *hakim*, and as the swing was pulled, out came the stomach worms from which he had been suffering for long.

Now one finds rope-swings only in the rural setting, barring a few which come up in the city and the resettlement colonies during the festival of *Teej* or in five-star hotels. Regharpura in Delhi used to have the largest number at one time, with girls swinging even on the busy roads. *Sawan* is said to be 'mast' and exercises an erotic pull on the young. So women were supposed to swing it off to the accompaniment of amorous songs. Now the grand swings of Agra, Delhi, Deeg, Alwar, Amber and Udaipur are all part of history.

25

A Market Full of Spices

The well after which Khari Baoli is named in Delhi was dug in the 17th century but it doesn't seem to exist now. The well had steps leading down to the water level so that people of Shahjahanabad could bathe and wash their clothes. But not many could have been allowed to dirty the water that way for even in those times there were rules of hygiene which were not violated by either the rich or the poor. However, the water was seldom used for drinking, because, as the name 'Khari' suggests, it was not sweet.

The well attracted merchants who sat under the shade of the trees that surrounded it and sold their wares. Most of them were grocers and in course of time a *kirana* market came up here. But that was centuries ago and those visiting Khari Baoli now will find it difficult to imagine that the place could once have been an open space where the citizens came to exercise themselves.

Passing by the market one can smell all the spices of the Indies. How many tons of them are stored in the shops is difficult to guess, but the very air is loaded with them. Even at night the place smells like the spice islands where the 'birds of paradise' came once a year to shed their feathers. You know, the spices of the East attracted European adventurers who wanted to tickle the Continental palate with something more than just boiled vegetables. Came the Dutch, the French and the British and eventually it was the East India Company which consolidated its hold on the country.

Standing in Khari Baoli, one is amazed at the role spices have played in the history of the world. They were in a way responsible for the discovery of America by Columbus, looking for a sea route to India and for Vasco da Gama finally making it via the Cape of Good Hope. You cannot ask a labourer in Khari Baoli about these things, but it was people like him at the ports who loaded bags of spices on ships which sailed away and brought back in return alien products and a culture which is now termed modern. So you see the link though not many are aware of it.

Khari Baoli is one of the biggest *kirana* markets in India and no wedding in the capital can be held without a visit to it, for it is here that one can get the best rice, oil, *ghee* and all the other condiments one needs for special lunch or dinner. Are the beautiful couples who glide down the road in the latest cars aware of this? Probably not, but they will by the time their children get married. And incidentally, there's a tablet in a gali here which states that Brig. Gen. Nicholson was shot from a nearby window by a sepoy in 1857.

26

The Shoe-Sellers' Riot

Shoe-sellers have occupied pride of place in Delhi bazars ever since the time of Shah Jehan. Before the Grand Moghul moved his capital to Delhi, the shoe trade was confined to Agra. Indeed that city is still the biggest manufacturer of shoes in the country and perhaps the world. The trade is mainly a cottage industry employing tens of thousands of workers. In Delhi the centre of the shoe industry is Ballimaran, an area which was once inhabited by boatmen.

During the reign of Mohammad Shah a peculiar incident took place in Delhi which has come to be known as the shoe-sellers' riot and resulted in one death at least – of a Haji – whose grave was built overnight in the middle of the road. It was on March 8, 1729 that a famous jeweller of Chandni Chowk, Sukh Karan was on his way home after meeting the emperor at the Red Fort. As he passed the shoe-sellers' street a cracker fired during the celebration of a festival damaged his clothes. Sukh Karan remonstrated with the revellers but they just laughed away his protest. On reaching home Sukh Karan sent his men to discipline the shoe-sellers. But they were outnumbered. Word reached the emperor, who was fond of Sukh Karan as the ornaments made by him pleased his concubines and also because he was generous in offering loans.

Though a drinking party was on at that time in the Rang Mahal, the emperor's nod was enough for some of his attendants to go to the aid of Sukh Karan. A big fight ensued and a stone struck one of the emperor's courtesans, who was on her way back to Chawri Bazar, where the dancing girls stayed in those days. Her accompanist hurled his *tabla* that broke the head of a shoe-seller. Gossip says the matter came up in the Dewan-e-Aam the next day. The courtesan who had been struck by a stone and lost a tooth was the prime witness and the shoe-sellers were punished with a fine. The sentence was as ingenious as it was frivolous. They had to supply shoes free of charge to every member of the harem for a full year.

Shoes in those days were mostly embroidered ones and worn by both men and women. But for the rich they were embroidered with gold and silver wire. The varieties were fantastic, especially for the begums whose 'zenani juti' was both dainty and handy to beat their outspoken maids with.

Figures for the 18th century are not available but in 1864 Delhi exported shoes worth Rs. 4 lakhs, which was a big amount considering the buying power of money in those days. The patent leather boot came with the advent of the British and slowly caught the fancy of Delhi's male population. But the Maratha shoe, with a heavy cleft-bound toe, continued to remain popular in regions under the control of Scindia and other Maratha chieftains.

The villagers then, as even now, were not fond of shoes but took them off and put them on their turbans to walk barefoot again. The zamindar, who needed three pairs of shoes a year, paid the village cobbler in grain at harvest time. Twelve annas was the cost of a good sturdy pair and Re. 1 for fancy shoes.

Coming back to the shoe-sellers' riot, it is interesting to note that it preceded the pigeon-sellers' riot that spread to the grain-sellers and led to the massacre of Delhi by Nadir Shah. But one wonders how Sukh Karan, a dandy of his times and fond of fancy shoes, eventally made up with the shoe-sellers. And also whether the latter were able to supply the Moghul harem with shoes for a year, which must have been a costly proposition, considering the large number of inmates. Or did they win over the emperor and escape with a lighter penalty? But surely the favourite courtesan's missing tooth must have long irked the colourful Mohammad Shah (Rangila Piya).

27

Lane of Royal Cooks near Jama Masjid

Abul Fazal had a voracious appetite, unlike his father, Sheikh Mubarak and brother, Faizi who, like him were among the Nine Jewels (*Nauratan*) of Akbar's court. It is said that 80 maunds of *khichri* was cooked on Abul Fazal's orders every day and anybody could just walk in and join in the meal.

At night the learned Abul Fazal, the emperor's friend, confidant and chronicler, who wrote the *Ain-e-Akbari*, would have 12 *seers* of delicious food placed on two tables, kept on either side of his bed, and whenever he got up he would eat, first from one side and then from the other. By morning there was nothing left. No wonder his wide girth is a prominent feature of Moghul paintings. But even so one marvels at the man's digestion.

There were other nobles who, though not as great eaters as Abul Fazal, were nevertheless fond of good food at breakfast, lunch and dinner – without being guilty of the sin of gluttony. Akbar himself was a frugal eater, though his son Jehangir ate well. Going by the popularity of *Mughlai* dishes in our age, it is not hard to guess that the Moghuls were connoisseurs of food too besides other things.

Most of us who like a tasty morsel can in moments of anticipation of a good meal, imagine delicious dishes being prepared, much like the Barmecide's Feast in the *Arabian Nights*. However, there have been people who frequented places – like the venue of a wedding or a party – where good food was being prepared to inhale the aroma, and one dare say some joined in the meal uninvited, like *Parak La Lambu*, who spent the day scouting for such places and went there in the evening as a 'guest'. Surely some such still survive.

There were many people too like the proverbial *Mullahji* who, being a miser, would have *niaz* (grace) said in front of somebody's marriage *pandal* where the smell of *pulao* filled the air, or before a sweetmeat seller, Dadaji's shop, rather than spend money on food and sweets in fulfilment of a wish, when pestered by friends. Hence the expression *Dadaji ki dukan pai niaz dilwange*.

Incidentally, there is a *gali* in Matia Mahal, near the Jama Masjid in Delhi, where reside a family of cooks whose forebears were around during the Moghul era. They are mostly old men who take contracts for marriages and other festive occasions because the younger generation has taken to other professions. The family occupation does not pay as much as it used to in days gone by.

Korma, rogan josh, tandoori murgh, biryani, kati kabab, gola kabab, shammi kabab, tandoori kabab, pulao-zarda, with *kheer* and *shahi tukre* are only some of the dishes which tickled the Moghul palate. All these are prepared by the cooks of Matia Mahal even now.

These Indian delicacies have charmed many dignitaries, and earned for the country the title of the 'land of gourmets'. And this is as it should be, for we have had such connoisseurs of food as Jehangir, Shah Jehan, Jahandar Shah, Mohammad Shah Rangila, Wajid Ali Shah and in our own times the Nawab of Rampur, Jawaharlal Nehru and Dr. Zakir Husain.

Despite his age, the last Moghul, Bahadur Shah Zafar retained his taste-bud and, besides the usual delicacies, the Mir Bakawal (head of the royal kitchen) saw to it that the menu included venison, quail, partridge and *haryal* (green pigeon).

The cooks of Matia Mahal do not prepare wild birds probably because tastes have changed and birds are hardly available in these times when wildlife is getting fast extinct. But they have their memories and when they talk of the good times, your mouth does start watering.

Where have the numerous cooking pots of Abul Fazal's household gone? One does not find any trace of them but at Bagh Farzana in Agra, which was laid by the nobleman's sister, Ladli Begum, a strange incident took place in the 19th century. The *bagh* was bought by a *seth* of Mathura and while digging was in progress, a body wrapped in a green cloth was recovered. But as soon as it came into contact with fresh air it disintegrated. Whatever remained was hastily reburied in the presence of Dr. Mukand Lal, assistant civil surgeon.

Soon after, one by one, all members of the *seth's* family died in quick succession. The incident was reported in The *Pioneer*, then published from Allahabad. Whose body was it? Ladli Begum's (she was a strikingly

Moghul cooks at work in a gali near Jama Masjid

beautiful woman, you know!) or of Abul Fazal himself? Nobody knows! But if anybody could have outdone the Romans of yore, it was this *Nauratan* who was as greedy for food as knowledge in times when he cooked and Akbar ate during hunting expeditions, replete with the wisecracks of Birbal. The palace named after the latter in Fatehpur Sikri was actually built for his daughter as the witty raja could not reside in the harem. His abode was Hans Mahal, now a ruin inundated by Jamuna water beyond Akbar's tomb at Sikandra. But Birbal was a sparse eater and the Lane of Royal Cooks is associated with Moghul gourmets of a later age.

28

Delhi's 'Agra Bazar'

If one were to look for a locale akin to Habib Tanvir's 'Agra Bazar' in Delhi, one would have to be satisfied with Tehraha Bahram Khan in the backyard of Daryaganj. Here under a huge tree sit people with baskets of seasonal fruit and vegetables and around them are petty shops whose owners hail one another and indulge in a little gaff when business is slack.

The Tehraha, at the convergence of three roads, is an old locality with houses that date back to the 18th century. Of course, it has nothing to do with Akbar's famous regent whose son, Abdul Rahim Khan-e-Khana, had palatial houses both at Delhi and Agra. But still Tehraha Behram Khan is a name of no small significance, with its own toughs, dandies, clowns, beggars and singing minstrels in the form of *sadhus* who come for a round early in the morning. They are followed by an occasional dervish or a kamliwallah baba, smoking a *bidi* through his shoulder and reciting an unintelligible but awe-inspiring 'Haq, haq, haq'.

There was a time when Chowk Hauz Qazi would have made a better comparison to Tanvir's locale, for here was a wider variety of life, complete with dancing girls in the nearby Chawri Bazar whose songs could be heard right up to the *chowk* on quiet nights after the last *tonga* had trotted off. The scene changed after Partition and now the only songs one hears here are of the filmi variety for the dancing girls are too far away to make an impact.

The *Roti Nama* and *Admi Nama* of Nazir Akbarabadi, alas, are no longer sung in the streets of Delhi. Even earlier it was only during the 'Urs' of Ajmer Sharif that pilgrims passing through the walled city were regaled by an old man in green shirt and *pyjamas* to the masterpieces of the poet, beating time with bangles and a small stick. It is said that Nazir's popularity in Delhi suffered because of the influence of Mir, Ghalib and Zauq, though the first two were also associated with Agra in their earlier years.

The man with the green shirt came singing down Urdu Bazar then turned into Matia Mahal, going past Chitli Qabar, Tehraha Bahram Khan, Kamra Bangash, Churiwalan, back to Jama Masjid and thence to the Chawri Bazar, Barshah Bulla and Hauz Qazi. Sometimes he branched into the lane that leads to Ballimaran, past Ghalib's house. But that was rare.

Coming back to the Tehraha with its monkeys and mutton shops huddled around the old mosque, one misses many old familiar faces. But it is some comfort that the new generation maintains the character of the three crossroads in Delhi's 'Agra Bazar'.

29

The Amazons of Delhi

Whenever the anniversary of the rebellion of 1857 comes around one cannot help thinking about it. There are so many places in Delhi which remind one of those times, particularly the area near the Kashmere Gate where a cinema now stands. There were huge trees here under which the sepoys rested or planned their attacks on the British troops stationed on the Ridge. Food was brought in huge vessels (*deghs*) for the freedom fighters and water was supplied by 'bhistis'. Still the arrangements left much to be desired and there were frequent quarrels over an extra share, though the meat served was not all mutton, the *rotis* thick and the rice coarse. But it must be remembered that to feed so many men even in those inexpensive times was not easy.

Sentries were posted on the walls of the Kashmere Gate who kept a sharp lookout for spies, Indian, of course, but working for the British. But as the siege of Delhi entered its final phase, the sepoys began to lose heart. It was during this period that 'The Fair Maid of Delhi' emerged. She was a big-built woman, with hardly any trace of beauty, who rode on horseback and struck terror in the hearts of the British soldiers. Sword-in-hand, she led the men on many a foray and even the emperor's sons and grandsons and the *purdah* ladies of Delhi came to witness her exploits.

Nobody now seems to remember who she was, and where she came from (probably Bareilly). But it is a well-known fact that some women in those days mastered the martial arts to defend the *zenana*. Among them were Pathan ladies, big hefty women who knew how to use the sword and spear, and could hold their own against an average soldier. One example that comes to mind in recent times is that of Mubarak, who however, is of negroid descent. Bent with age now, in her youth she and her sisters, Hasina and Amina, guarded a *nawab's zenana* for years and beat the daylights out of any intruder. Mubarak, who went away to Dehra Dun, must be 100 years old now if alive. Hasina and Amina died in Agra long ago.

Besides 'The Fair Maid of Delhi' there were other women who were equally brave. The two 'hags' from Rampur, particularly have been described by some historians as the 'real leaders' of the demoralized sepoys whom they taunted into action. It was near the Kashmere Gate that a party of British soldiers was fired upon with such ferocity that they nearly retreated. But one of them noticed some movement in a tree and fired back. Down came the sniper and it was a woman.

Sad to say the women who played such a vital role in the defence of Delhi were forgotten all too soon by its inhabitants. No memorials were raised to them even after the country attained independence. But it is still not too late to honour them. Perhaps some old family in the walled city may even supply their names for a tablet to be installed outside the Kashmere Gate on May 11 next, for it was on that day that the Mutiny broke out in Delhi!

FAITH & PIETY

30

Where Girls Pray:
Mazar of Bibi Fatima

The mystic experience is not limited to men, for women too are partakers of it – even though men outnumber them. The same is true of the Sufis, many of whom trace their origin to Hazrat Khizr, who is believed to have been one of those who survived the Deluge and later served as a pathfinder to Moses when he led the Israelites through the desert. Maulana Rumi was influenced by him, so also Khwaja Moinuddin Chisti and the others of his 'silsila'. Bibi Fatima, who was a contemporary of Baba Farid Ganjshakar and Hazrat Nizamuddin Auliya, too sought the support of Hazrat Khizr's mantle.

Bibi Fatima belonged to Saam, a place on the Iraqi-Irani border, but came to India in response to an inner urge. She eventually settled down in Delhi, where she died. Her shrine is situated in Bapa Nagar (near Kaka Nagar), a most unlikely locality for such a tomb. But in the 13th century there was no Bapa Nagar and the place was a wilderness, far removed even from the seat of government of the Slave dynasty, founded by Qutbuddin Aibak, who had been bought as a slave by Mohammad Ghori or Mohammad bin Sam.

Fariduddin Attar in his famous work, *Mantiq-at-Tayr* or the *Parliament of Birds*, likens the soul to a bird which has to pass through seven valleys: those of Search, Love, Mysticism, Detachment, Unity, Bewilderment, and Final Annihilation – before it reaches the gates of the Almighty. Something like that was stated by the Venerable Bede, the 8th century Christian monk, who compared human life to a bird which comes in through the dark, flies through a lit-up hall and then goes into the darkness again. The

Begum Fatima's *mazar*

darkness signifies eternity with a brief interlude of mortal existence before the ultimate reunion with the eternal.

Bibi Fatima's article of faith was also based on the belief of the final meeting with the Great Beloved – God. It is noteworthy that she did not ever marry but passed her life in the love of Allah through meditation and mystic experience. To those who came to her she was guide, philosopher and friend. Her 'mureeds' were both men and women.

Those who revere her say that the Bibi led a dual existence. Outwardly she was calm and did not betray the inner turmoil of the spiritual yearning for the Supreme. Did she come to India alone or with her family at a time when distances were long and people travelled on horseback or in caravans? Some say that she came as an infant with her parents, others that she accompanied only her father and yet others that she was conceived in Saam but born here. She lived a very long time ago, you know. But it is worth noting that Nizamuddin Auliya called her 'Apa', a term used for an elder sister and to Baba Farid she was like a younger sister or daughter.

They visited her out-of-the-way abode after hearing reports of her piety and spiritual eminence, though according to some they had come to know of her presence though their own meditation and 'Jalal'. But Bibi Fatima was a simple woman who did not show off her saintliness. Her frugal existence was akin to what is so well expressed in Rumi's *Mathnawi*:

> Treat your fears and despair as the voices of the deceitful Satan who is out to delude you into depression and worries. Any sound that pulls you upwards, necessarily issues forth from the higher spiritual regions. Every sound that drags you down in the mire of fears and temptations, take it as the howl of wolves that tear men into pieces.

The Bibi was a spiritual recluse for whom religion was just an outer covering because a Sufi is different from a mere adherent of faith for whom only fasting, prayer and good works constitute the good life. The *Sufiana Kalaam* goes beyond this, for mysticism is a wide robe which transcends earthly bounds and is not subservient to limitations of time and space. The wanderings of the mind and spirit are limitless and it is thus that the true Sufi is constantly attuned to the eternal.

One visits the shrine of this hoary woman saint with great expectations but is disappointed at the way it is maintained. The caretakers are handicapped by lack of resources and those who should help hold back their hand. It would be in the fitness of things if the Archaeological Department takes it under its protective wing, for it is a historic place. The Delhi Administration could also help by releasing funds for the upkeep of the tomb of the first Sufi woman saint of India whose followers belong to all communties.

Burqa-clad women and those with vermilion in their hair pray side by side at this inter-faith shrine. Bibi Fatima's 'Urs' is held at her death anniversary in February every year. How she died nobody seems to know nor how the grave became a shrine with a green cloth covering it. That the Bibi fulfils vows, especially in regard to young girls seeking husbands is a deep-seated belief. Others swear that she has come to their aid at times of great distress. Such a saint certainly needs a befitting monument.

31

Matka Pir
Hazrat Azmat Sheikh

The 'Urs' of Hazrat Azmat Sheikh Abu Bakr Tartoushi Hadri Kalandari draws a large number of people of all communities. The shrine of Matka Shah Baba, as he is popularly known, is situated near Pragati Maidan, on the Delhi-Mathura Road. He is believed to have been a contemporary of Hazrat Qutubuddin Bakhtiar Kaki, having come to India from Tartous, in Syria, after the invasion of Mohammad Ghori.

The Saint was held in high esteem by Qutbuddin Aibak (1206-1210) and his successor Altamash, whose daughters Razia and Sazia were also among the devotees. When Chingez Khan invaded India in 1221 in pursuit of Shah Jalaluddin of Khwarizan, the people of Delhi were greatly alarmed and so was Sultan Altamash. Jalaluddin had asked the Slave ruler for asylum, which he wisely refused, saying that the climate of Delhi would not suit him.

Was this done on the advice of the saint, who is said to have told Altamash not to worry, for if the fugitive was kept away the great Khan and his horsemen would just disappear? And this is exactly what happened, for Chingez passed like a storm through Punjab, stopping briefly on the banks of the Indus where Jalaluddin made his last stand. He lost but managed to escape by jumping into the river, along with his horse in a feat which astonished even the Mongol warlord.

Altamash, besides being a great conqueror and consolidator, was also a patron of art and literature at whose court poets like Malik Tajuddin and Ruhani and litterateures like Mihaj-e-Siraj flourished. At the same time he befriended holy men like Khwaja Qutbuddin and Hazrat Azmat

*Matka*s at the shrine

Sheikh and sought their counsel in matters of state and before launching his military expeditions.

His success against such powerful rivals as Nasiruddin Qubacha, Governor of Multan and Sindh, and Tajuddin Yaldoz, Governor of Ghazni, are attributed as much to his fighting skill as to divine help.

Hazrat Azmat Sheikh, whose home-town Tartous today occupies an area of 1,892 sq km with a population of about 500,000 came to India via Punjab and settled down in Delhi in response to a spiritual urge. In those days the city of Delhi as we know it now did not exist. Everything was centred in Mehrauli and the saint's 'khankha' or hospice was far removed from it. But it was close enough to the Jamuna and just a stone's throw from the Bhairon Mandir dating back to the time of the Mahabharata.

There are many stories about how the saint came to be known as Matka Baba. According to one of them, a man and his wife came to seek his help for the birth of a son. As they were very poor they had brought only a *chatty* or *matka* full of chick-pea and jaggery to offer to the holy man. The saint asked them to put the *matka* in the courtyard and leave the rest to God. After a year the couple came again but this time with a bonny boy. Their wish had been fulfilled and they offered another *matka*. Since then people started making that sort of offering.

Matka Baba performed many miracles before his death in AD 1235. Altamash too died in the same year and at about the same time Hazrat Nizamuddin Auliya was born. Rukn-ud-Din Firoz ascended the throne with the help of his despotic mother, Shah Tukran, and hatched a conspiracy to kill his sister Razia. But both mother and son were assassinated and Razia was chosen Sultan. The believers think that it was because of the blessing of the saint that his devotee, a woman at that, was able to achieve the distinction of becoming the ruler of Hindustan. But that subsequently she *belied* expectations was due to her own faults rather than a reflection on the saint's capacity to give continued protection.

This is the 774th year of the death of Matka Shah Baba but people from all walks of life still flock to his shrine. And they still offer *matkas* filled with *matar* (chick-pea) and *gur* (jaggery). The contents are distributed to the poor and the *matkas* are left at the shrine, which is now full of them. They are to be seen everywhere – even on walls and trees.

The 'Urs' which is held in December is notable for the fact that among those who offer the first *chuddars* and *matkas* are the *mahant* of Bhairon temple and a Hindu businessman. This is followed by a *langar* or public feeding and there are *qawwalis* which go on till late at night. The story that the shrine was the creation of the British to exploit minority sentiments is a latter-day development in which some see the hand of ultra-orthodox elements.

The *langars* and *qawwalis* are the main features on the second day too. The 'Urs' ends with the 'kul' ceremony presided over by the Sajjadanashin, Pir Mohammad Naseem Sultan Kalandari, the hereditary keeper of the shrine. It is a far cry from the days of Altamash to our times, but the respect in which Matka Baba is still held is to be seen to be believed.

32

The Legacy of a Pir

Sunehri Bagh Masjid on Rafi Marg, New Delhi, doesn't look like a mosque at all, for it has no dome and is more like a house with a double storey. A long time ago, probably when Shahzada Ali Gohur was yet to begin his reign as Shah Alam, a saintly man – a Pir – constructed this mosque in the area which was then known as Sunheri village.

Some say the village was named after a Pathan who was called Sunher Khan because of his complexion and there are others who think it got its name from the golden wheat crop that was harvested in it or because of a princess who enjoyed that pseudonym. But the village is no longer there, for when Lutyens laid his New Delhi the rural homes and fields disappeared and the villagers were shunted off to the trans-Jamuna area.

The Pir, who was known as Sayyid Sahib, a designation given to those who are connected with the family of the Prophet, built the mosque with the help of the villagers without any patronage from the rich. The architecture was different from the regal creations of the age and more in tune with the needs of the villagers. They wanted both a prayer house and a community centre, and that was what the Pir gave them. So they must have been happy with their effort.

Today Sunheri Bagh Masjid stands amidst modern buildings, a stone's throw from Parliament House. Many MPs offer prayers in it and their patronage helps to keep the mosque in an excellent state of preservation. A cycle repair shop, a tea stall and a *dhaba* or eating house also function here. And the prayer chamber being on top means that the sanctity of the mosque is not disturbed. Seeing the number of those attending prayers on a Friday or in the evening one should think the masjid does not lack in popularity. People coming on errands from the walled city and those who visit New Delhi for sight-seeing or business find it convenient for carrying out their devotions.

But what about the descendants of those who built the mosque and lived in Sunheri village before it was demolished? From all accounts they have not forgotten the place and do visit it occasionally to maintain the old link with their Pir Sahib who left a legacy for them in the shape of the unconventional masjid.

33

Drinking to the Deity

Can one offer liquor at a temple? This is exactly what people do when they visit the Bhairon Mandir near the Purana Quila in Delhi. The bottles are opened before the deity and then taken away for consumption. The priest supposedly will have none of it. And what would he do with the cocktail offered? Sell it? There is rum, whisky, gin, brandy, country liquor and any other brand that you can think of to appease Bhairon for a wish fulfilled or a boon sought. The *devata* is both protector of his devotees and averter of tragedies. His blessings are needed by all those who practise the tantric arts.

It is believed that Bhimsen, the second eldest of the Pandava brothers, brought the idol of Bhairon from Varanasi for the protection of their fort. The deity told him in a dream that he should not be dirty in any sense while carrying the idol on its long journey to Delhi. The moment he defiled himself in any way, nature's call included, Bhairon would make his home at that very spot and not proceed further.

The mighty warrior that he was, Bhim was able to control his bodily functions right up to the time he reached the walls of the fort. But before he could enter it through the small gate, that existed near the site where the temple stands, he could not control himself anymore. Having brains as well as brawn, he picked up the stone idol and put it on the wall before going to ease himself. And true to his warning Bhairon stayed put at that spot as a *dwarpal*, a guardian of the gate. In later centuries when the place became a wilderness tantrics must have had a field day there.

Bhairon is believed to be the bodyguard of the *Devi* and follows her wherever she goes. Some say he is the principal server of Shiva while others assert that he is attached to the god of death Yama. As such Kal

Bhairon is worshipped as an intercessor. However, there are people who repose complete faith in him and even dedicate their lives to the service of Bhairon.

Sadhus who do so are known as Bhairon baba and go about with a primitive bagpipe, bells tinkling at their waist and feet. When dressed in the supposed manner of Bhairon they do not stop even for a minute. While pausing to take alms or for some other reason, they keep moving their feet like one jogging at slow speed. No wonder their calves are well developed, along with their bodies, for they are a tough-looking lot with piercing eyes and a fiery temper.

Most of those who visit the Bhairon temple, now well renovated and maintained, whether they are rich or poor, offer a bottle of liquor. This is in keeping with the nature of the deity to whom nothing is taboo.

34

Site of Secret Ritual

There is a mosque-like structure near New Delhi station which, gossip says, marks the site of the prayer house where the *thugs* took their secret oath in the 18th century. Things have changed a great deal since then and the fearsome band of men who practised *thugee* no longer pose a danger to society, their place having been taken by the modern-day desperadoes. Still, those who claim to be in the know cannot think of them without a shudder.

It is on record that during the 14th century 1,000 *thugs* were captured and hung in the streets of Delhi. And, 200 years later, Sher Shah Suri organized a cavalry of 1,200 men to keep them at bay. Akbar and his successors also launched widespread drives against the *thugs*, though it was only in the 19th century that Sir W.H. Sleeman succeeded in wiping them out after a relentless operation lasting seven years. Sleeman insinuated that the *thugs* were close to Nizamuddin Auliya and paid annual tribute to him at the mosque he frequented.

The *thugs* used to travel to Delhi before Dussehra, and the oath-taking took place just after Ravana and his kinsmen had met their preordained fate. Ceremony over, the recruits were taught the secret vocabulary known as *Ramasee*, which consisted of phrases like 'Ali Khan Bhai Salaam', a sign of mutual recognition. Later a *guru*, an expert strangler, would teach them the art of throwing the handkerchief, known as the 'roomal' round the victim's neck. It was a large piece of cloth and a sharp wrench with it killed the victim in an instant, without the slightest noise. But for this they had to wait for the 'phirnee' or good omen and the command word 'paan' (execution).

Thugs overpowering a victim

Meer Sahib Ameer Ali, who alone killed nearly 900 people, had acquired such mastery in throwing the 'roomal' that the victim was dead before his body hit the ground. Ameer Ali was born at Morena, near Agra, and brought up by a group of *thugs* who had killed his father and mother while they were on their way to Indore. Ameer became such a notorious *thug* that his name struck terror even in the hearts of the officers sent out against him. A huge reward was announced for his capture and he was finally betrayed by his own men. Ameer Ali, however, turned approver and saved his neck from the gallows.

In his confessions to Col. Meadows Taylor of the Nizam's dominions, Ameer Ali mentions visits to Delhi for the initiation ceremony of the recruits, and the masjid where they stayed. The *thugs*, incidentally, were both Muslims and Hindus who worshipped Kali, the goddess of destruction. It is interesting to note that people of the lower castes and lepers, *nanbais*, barbers and Sikhs were never killed by the *thugs*. Women too were generally spared and also eunuchs and the handicapped.

Just imagine bands of *thugs* buying cloth for their *roomals* from the markets of Delhi and then hurrying to the prayer house to take the secret oath of Kali. Now, as trains whistle past, few know what used to go on at the site subsequently occupied by New Delhi station.

35

Kalkaji Temple

The Kali Temple in Kalkaji boasts of a history that goes back 3,000 years, although the oldest existing portion of it (built by a *seth*) dates to 1764-1771 when the Marathas were in power and the Moghul ruler of Delhi, Shah Alam, was a puppet in their hands. However, the couplet (*Az Dilli ta Palam Badshah Shah Alam*) denoting that the extent of his dominion extended from Delhi to Palam had not gained currency yet. That was to come later. Still in effect he had very little power even then and the Marathas were able to restore many old temples and shrines which had been lying neglected during the Muslim rule.

Looking at the present-day Kalkaji temple one may find it hard to believe that this shrine to Kali is an antique one, where perhaps even the Pandavas and Kauravas had worshipped during the reign of Yudhishtira, whose citadel of Indraprastha had the fabled fairy gates of which bards sang, much like Homer of old, right up to the time of Prithviraj Chauhan. Folklore is replete with tales of the Kalkaji Temple, so much so, that one does no know where legend ends and history begins.

One story says that a king who had lost several battles to an invader took shelter at the spot where he lost his army. Tired and exhausted after the battle in the day, he fell asleep and dreamt of the goddess Kali asking him to try his luck again. When the king got up in the morning, he found to his surprise that the troops he thought he had lost had returned. He led them to battle again and succeeded in routing the enemy. But despite his heady success he did not forget the goddess and built a temple in her honour. Situated about 14 km from Delhi proper, the temple still has an idol of Kali, draped in red silk brocade, which is enclosed by a marble railing. People flock to it in large numbers every Tuesday, when a small fair springs up near the temple. But the big fairs are held on the 8th day of Chait and Asad, the first one after Holi and the second just before the beginning of the rainy month of *Sawan*.

Small red flags decorate the temple and women out-number men among the devotees. Could it be that the king whose life and domain Kali had saved had been influenced by his queen to build the shrine? On considering the fact that monarchs are generally forgetful in such matters one would not be surprised if it were so. But then there are other tales too about the origin of the temple and one doesn't know how to sift fact from gossip.

36

Bela's Samadhi

Atop a mound behind the cremation ground in Jhandewalan Extension is believed to be the *samadhi* of Bela Sidhi. Bela was the daughter of Prithviraj Chauhan who committed *sati* after her husband was killed in a battle that was fought in the area between Panchkuian Road and what is now Pusa Institute. The place was then cut off by a rocky terrain and the battle raged nearly the whole day. Late in the evening word was brought to the Rajput ladies waiting under a clump of trees that the chieftain was dead and the battle lost. What his name was is not known nor that of his adversary. It was because of Bela that her husband could lay some claim to fame and it is she who is the riddle of our curiosity.

To enter a realm of controversy, it was for Bela that Prithviraj Chauhan is supposed by some to have built the Qutb Minar, so that she could view the Jamuna every day as she dried her long hair in the morning sunshine. Conceding this claim with apologies to Qutbuddin Aibak and his successor Altamash, one can picture the young Bela busy with her coiffure amidst her maids of honour. It must have been an elaborate process for the princess who had her hair combed tight and then made into a pigtail with a 'tika' or 'jhoomer', perhaps encrusted with a diamond in this case, conspicuous on the forehead and then an 'odhni' to cover the head.

Bela is a beautiful flower according to an old lullaby, greatly loved by God (and men of course) which had to sacrifice its life because the Maker wanted it for his celestial garden. Princess Bela named after the flower must have been beautiful too. And she also sacrificed her life for her lord and master. This act of hers has not been forgotten for a *mela* used to be held at the *samadhi* of the princess where women came from far and near to pay homage to a chaste and loving wife and a great *sati*.

Climbing up the mound and talking to the old *sadhu* standing under the shade of two *peepul* trees, one is transported to medieval times, even though it is hard to swallow the claim that the trees date back to that period. But then the *sadhu* has his own brand of history, according to which Bela was the daughter-in-law of Prithviraj Chauhan's grand-daughter, though he conceded that she too committed *sati*. Could it be that Bela was commemorated by successive princesses after her? Be that as it may, the *samadhi* legend has come down from pre-Moghul times, probably the Sultanate period. The belief is strengthened by the fact that a *mandir*, which marks the site where Bela is said to have committed *sati*, still stands in Jhandewalan.

It is strange that hardly any building of note was erected in the Karol Bagh area during the heyday of the Moghuls. Construction was confined to the northern and southern parts of the capital. In those days the Ridge cut off most of this area and for a long time it remained isolated. The name Jhandewalan was given during Shah Jehan's reign, though prayer flags, *Jhandas*, had been offered at the Devi temple prior to that too. It has perhaps been renovated on the pattern of the Vaishnodevi shrine and is today the object of much devotion.

The construction of such temples followed a dream in which the *Devi* commanded that her idol be installed and worshipped. Sometimes the dream came to several neighbours, and at times it was the raja who dreamt it.

Animal sacrifices to the *Devi* were a common ritual. That such sacrifices took place in Jhandewalan is evident from the thicket behind the temple area, much of which has been cut down to accommodate flatted factories. Even as lately as the second decade of the 20th century, Jhandewalan was a forlorn place. *Badmashes* made it difficult for women to venture there after sunset and so offerings were made only in the day, when armed men accompanied them. Now the women who come for 'darshan' need no escort (unless they need one to guard against chain-snatchers). The 'thali' offered contains, besides other things, a 'chunri' or veil and bangles. Red is the colour that predominates, though the bangles are generally green. The *pujari* receives the 'thali' and gives a small portion of its contents as 'prasad' to the devotee who has to hurry out, content in the thought that nothing escapes the all-seeing eye of the *Devi*. Bela too was blessed by her.

37

Gurdwara in the Palace of Raja Jai Singh

What was once the bungalow of Mirza Raja Jai Singh of Amber has over the centuries become Gurdwara Bangla Sahib. The Delhi palace of Jai Singh, general of Emperor Aurangzeb, was surrounded by a beautiful garden with pleasure walks and a *sarovar* or pool in the centre. During Haryali *Teej*, Rajput princesses and their maids used to swing there. And during Diwali the bungalow used to glitter in the light of thousands of lamps.

Raja Jai Singh was a man of taste, even though he was one of the greatest warlords of his time. He owned some of the best horses and his armoury was the envy of every man who wielded the sword. There were beautiful women in his *zanana* who danced and sang every evening. But early in the morning the Raja used to ride away to the Red Fort where the emperor took counsel with him on matters of statecraft and warfare.

But Jai Singh was a busy man who did not stay put in Delhi. Most of the time he was fighting wars at the head of the Moghul army or quelling rebellions. It was his help that Aurangzeb took in dealing with the Marathas and the Sikhs, both of whom had been alienated by the emperor.

Even a peaceful Guru like Har Rai, who had succeeded Guru Hargovind, drew the emperor's ire for the alleged help he gave to the fugitive Dara Shikoh during the war of succession that followed Shah Jehan's illness. Guru Har Rai sent his elder son Ram Rai to talk things over with the emperor and later his younger son, Harkrishan was brought to the court with the help of Jai Singh. Harkrishan, who had succeeded his father as the child *Guru*, lived at the palace of Jai Singh about the year 1664 and held discussions there with the Moghul heir apparent, Prince

Palace of Raja Jai Singh

Muazzam (later Bahadur Shah I). But the Guru died soon after under mysterious circumstances. Some say he was a victim of smallpox, but the general belief is that he was done away with on the orders of Aurangzeb.

The palace of Jai Singh became the headquarters of his descendant, Jai Singh II, while the latter was building the Jantar Manter (1724-25) during the reign of Mohammad Shah. It was eventually acquired by the Sikh *panth* and converted into a *gurdwara*.

The building which has come up as Bangla Sahib makes one wonder how history repeats itself. It was at the site of the pleasure garden of Jai Singh's forbear, Raja Man Singh, that the Taj Mahal was built because it was found to be the most suitable place in Agra. And here in Delhi the site of the bungalow of Mirza Raja Jai Singh has made way for another monument.

The Rajput connexion links the Taj and Bangla Sahib and the full moon sheds its lustre on them on *Purnima* nights. Both buildings reflect its glory, one on the banks of the Jamuna and the other around the *sarovar* which dates back to near-medieval times.

38

Rakabganj Gurdwara:
When Nature Frowned

Gurdwara Rakabganj is one of those shrines of the Capital which are reminders of strange happenings. Passing by it on a sunny afternoon one may think that it is just another place of worship. But actually it is not, because to those who know it brings to mind a night similar to the one in Rome when the conspirators gathered to plan the murder of Caesar; followed the storm and the weird darkness in which the very trees seemed to moan and groan; and the warlord's wife, though disturbed in her sleep, dreamt of his impending assassination.

Well that sort of night was experienced in Chandni Chowk in the reign of Aurangzeb several centuries after Caesar. It followed the execution of Guru Tegh Bahadur on the Emperor's orders in a battle of egos. But they say a terrible storm (*Kali Andhi*) struck the Capital just then. May be it was a tornado which swept everything before it.

The Moghul soldiers on guard lost their bearings and while they were still trying to recover their wits, a man called Jaita took them by surprise, and picking up the head of the guru fled into the gloomy night. Simultaneously, Lakhi Shah, a contractor of the Moghul court, came with horses and bullocks, driven by his eight sons, and carried away the body lying below a tree, under cover of darkness.

They drove past the Red Fort and on to their house which was situated amid the wilderness of Raisina hill, for even in those days many of the well-to-do lived beyond the city limits. The body and the house were both set on fire so that it looked like a conflagration from a distance in times when one could see the Qutub from any rooftop in Shahjahanabad. With none suspecting their motives they were able to collect the remains of the guru and put them in an urn and bury it where the house stood.

The head was, of course, taken away to Anandpur in Punjab where it was cremated separately. But that was not part of the adventure of Lakhi Shah and his burly sons who had grown strong on the milk of many cows.

Today the site of the house which was set on fire is marked by Gurdwara Rakabganj. The name Rakabganj is common to localities in North India, some of them associated with mosques or the sale of utensils, particularly plates (*rakabis*). But this one is different in that it brings to mind the strange evening on November 11, 1675 when nature frowned on a ruthless act.

39

Abode of the Matas near Rouse Avenue

How often monuments spring up at places associated with great personages and things is remarkable. Take the Mata Sundari Gurdwara near Rouse Avenue in New Delhi. It marks the site of the house where Guru Gobind Singh lived in the 18th century. Mata Sundari and Mata Sahib Devi survived the 10th and last guru by 28 years and 30 years, respectively.

They also resided for some time near Ajmeri Gate in Kucha Dilwali Singhan during the decadent years of the Moghul empire, when Mohammad Shah was on the throne, but luckily did not live to see the sack of Delhi by Nadir Shah.

Guru Gobind Singh came to Delhi a number of times, staying for a short while before proceeding on his missionary travels. After the death of Aurangzeb when the war of succession broke out between Prince Muazzam and Prince Azam, the former sought the help of Gobind Singh who sent a token force to help his friend at the battle of Jajua, near Agra, in June 1707. But the guru camped nearby and when the need arose for reinforcements, he rushed in to Muazzam's aid, Azam was fatally wounded and his elder brother ascended the throne as Shah Alam, Bahadur Shah I.

When Guru Gobind Singh wanted to felicitate the emperor, he shot an arrow into the walls of the Red Fort and Bahadur Shah knew that his friend had arrived. After the death of the guru and then of the emperor, Jahandar Shah came to the throne and lasted just a year, followed by Farukhseyer, two other puppets, and then Mohammad Shah Rangila. But Mata Sundari and Mata Sahib Devi were not unduly disturbed, except in June 1725 when they had to leave Delhi and live in Mathura for two years and earlier when the heroic Banda was executed.

They continued to guide the *panth* from Mata Sundari Haveli, sending *hukumnamas* (encyclicals) to followers as far away as Kabul in the north and Dhaka in the east, rallying the Sikhs and prevailing upon them not to accept those who were trying to set up an 11th guru.

Their abode, built in 1727, is now a *gurdwara* and there is a college and road too named after Mata Sundari said to be one of the most beautiful women of her time. Those who come to worship at this shrine remember the venerable ladies who, despite the loss of four sons early in life, left an indelible mark on Delhi when it was passing through some of its most troublesome times. The two travelled on camel carts, bullock carts and in palanquins to propagate the message they had imbibed so well.

40

Mast Qalandar

In the ruins of the Kotla lived a *Mast Qalandar*. Every day he would walk down to the tomb of Bhure Shah in the vicinity of the Red Fort and pray to the "saint with the fiery temper". A big-built man with a barrel of a chest and a shaggy beard, his prayers were not the silent outpourings of a heart but the mutterings of one who had lost contact with his surroundings and lived in a world of his own. He would walk down to the shrine of Hare-Bhare and beat his 'chimta' (iron tongs) to announce his arrival.

The young were overawed by him and the old considered him to be someone from the past who had been visiting the Jama Masjid area for as long as one cared to remember. Like Zanoni, he was likened to an order of mystics who thrive for centuries.

Rafiq Khan, for whom illiteracy was a great boon because it marginalized logic, had this tale to tell about the *Mast Qalandar*: When Firoz Shah took the reins of government into his hands after the sudden death of Mohammad bin Tughlak in Sind, he was reminded by a young *fakir* that the emperor had died not because of the after-effects of a dish of bad fish but because of cruelty to his subjects. So it was Firoz's lot to undo the harm done by his cousin. The new Sultan was somehow impressed by the words of the *fakir* and brought him along to Delhi. And when he built his Kotla a special place was marked in it as the *fakir's* abode.

Firoz Shah died after a long reign. Taimur came and devastated Delhi. The Tughlaks were ousted by the Sayyids, who in turn lost their kingdom to the Lodhis. Next came the Moghuls and the British but the *fakir* was still around. So many dynasties had come and gone but he contined to live in the Kotla and visit the Jama Masjid every afternoon. During the Mutiny he was at the Kashmiri Gate, encouraging the *bhistis* to carry water to the sick and wounded sepoys and after Delhi fell into the hands of the British again, he was back on his daily rounds.

The *Mast Qalandar* was seen right up to 1947 but after the riots he just disappeared. Some said that he had migrated to Pakistan and others that he had decided to make himself scarce because of the disgusting events, for nobody could even imagine that he might have been killed – such was the aura that surrounded him.

Abdul Hai, whose religious and other beliefs are tinged more by logic and reason than blind faith, had a more plausible story to offer. The *Mast Qalandar* was a member of an order of dervishes who lived in secluded areas, and what was better than the ruins of the Kotla? Even if a *Mast Qalandar* had met Firoz Tughlak in Sind, it did not mean that he continued to live right up to 1947. Yes members of that order were pretty common up to that time but there was no question of immortality attached to them. You can still find them visiting the Jama Masjid, area especially during the Ajmer 'Urs', when some of them strike strident poses at the grave of Hare-Bhare, shouting 'Maula Bhej, Bhej' meaning 'send money to visit Ajmer – or I'll break this shrine'. To supplement their threat they either lift up their 'chimta' or pick up a huge stone. But somebody or the other always fulfils their wish and so the threat (sic) is warded off.

It is generally assumed that the order of *Mast Qalandars* originated in Iran, where before the advent of Islam it was almost unkown. It came to India with the Arab invasion of Sind and its adherents spread as far as Bengal. *Mast Qalandars* entered South India too some time in the 13th century, but in Delhi they have existed since the time of the Slave dynasty. Some, however, claim that the order was mostly of Afghan origin.

One remembers a *Mast Qalandar* who used to stand in front of the sweet shop of Haji Kalan and beat his back with a 'chimta' from time to time. He wore a huge black shirt and was quite wild in his habits, but people were somehow attracted to him though he hardly seemed to care and the more alms he got the wilder he became, like the one mentioned by Ahmed Ali in his "Twilight in Delhi". He used to come all the way from Basti Nizamuddin on foot and lived in one of the ruined *dargahs*. But he is long dead. However, the Archaeological Department sees to it that none of these *fakirs* sets up abode in the Kotla. But a *Mast Qalandar* cell there might help to attract more tourists to the Kotla, which in any case lies deserted most of the time.

41

Delhi's Parsi Connexion

Parsis came to North India over 500 years ago, though some think it was much earlier. But historically speaking, the Parsi association with Delhi dates back to the time of Akbar, when Dastur Meherjirana of Navsari impressed the emperor with his piety and knowledge. Thereafter, other learned Parsis were invited to Akbar's new capital of Fatehpur Sikri, where they took part in religious discourse with Hindu, Jain, Muslim and Christian scholars.

It can be conjectured that Parsi buildings must have been in existence at Agra and Delhi even in those times, but no trace of them remains now. However, an inscription bears testimony to the fact that the site of the old *aramgah* (cemetery) in Delhi was acquired by Jamsetjee Cavesjee Jussawala in 1869 when the doyen of Moghul poets, Ghalib, was still alive. This link in the Parsi connection with the Capital grew with the formation of the 'Parsi Anjuman' in 1925, an event in its own right because in 1913 there were hardly 30 or 40 Parsis in Delhi. Their number now is about 1,000.

Did the Tower of Silence ever exist in Delhi? No, but just as one leaves Delhi Gate and enters Bahadur Shah Zafar Marg, a signboard with the words 'Delhi Parsi Anjuman' greets the eye and therein hangs a tale. Behind the board in a compound are the Mehgusi Parsi Dharamshala, or rest house, the Bhiwandiwalla (community) Hall, located within the premises of the Anjuman, which also houses books on Zoroastrianism, its history and culture, and the Kaikhusuru Palonji Katrak Dar-e-Meher or Fire Temple.

There are three kinds of fire temples: Atash Behram, Atash Adarn, Agvary or Dar-e-Meher and the Atash Dadgah or the household fire in every Parsi home. The first fire temple in India was consecrated in AD 790

Fire Temple

at Sanjan from the *alat* (instruments) brought by the Parsis from Khorasan. Hence, the importance of Delhi's one and only Fire Temple.

For the curious visitor viewing the Dar-e-Meher from outside, the history of the Parsi community comes to mind. Its origins go back to the Iranians who ruled as early as 3000 BC, though the religion propagated by the prophet Zarathushtra flourished in Iran until the defeat of the Sassanian king Yazdegard III by the Arabs at the battle of Nihavand in AD 641. More than 100 years later, in AD 766 the first Parsis landed on the Kathiwar coast to escape persecution. Since then they have lived in the land of their adoption.

Every day when the liturgy is performed at the Fire Temple the names and deeds of the great saints and kings of Iran are remembered. And as the early morning breeze blows in from the Jamuna, the beautiful dawn prayer *Hosh-Baam* is recited. The opening line, 'Through Asha most high, Asha most pure', seem to merge with the first rays of the sun, for it is the sanctity of light that the temple personifies.

In a way it reflects the glory of Ahura Mazda, the supreme deity. Ahura means Lord and Mazda, the wise or one full of light – the first and the last. Along with Ahura Mazda there are six other Ahuras, explains a Parsi worshipper at the temple. These are his six angels, who are also known as the six cardinal virtues, through whom only Ahura Mazda can be worshipped (Spenta Mainya, vice-regent of God). This is borne out by the *Avesta*, the sacred scriptures, and the *Gathas*.

The six *Ahuras*, according to the theologian Sydney Cave, are *Asha*, the Right, or Truth, or Righteousness; *Vohu Manah*, Good Thought; *Khshathra*, Dominion; *Aramaiti*, Piety, female counterpart of Dominion; *Haurvatat*, Welfare; and *Ameretat*, Immortality. The importance of the Fire Temple can be gauged from the fact that Parsis prefer to put their dead bodies in the Towers of Silence so that birds may devour them. To bury them would be to defile the earth and burning would pollute the fire, the most sacred of all elements. The fire in the Atash Temple is never extinguished, reveals the worshipper. It is considered regal, with a crown hanging over the cauldron, three feet in diameter and four feet high. The fire in it is fed by a priest five times a day and on special occasions with small wood. As one walks out of the Atash Temple compound, one is filled with awe and wonder at the sacredness of the place that leads from darkness to light. However, in places like Delhi and Agra (where there is no Tower of Silence), Parsis have *aramgahs*, where the dead are laid to rest. These places are named after their heroes like Rustam, whose names are also recited every morning.

42

Still Surviving on Gossip

Ludlow Castle is no more, but the street to which it lent its name, though known as Raj Niwas Marg now, is still buzzing with memories of the days when the British had their famous Delhi Club here. The castle has made way for a school and the hackney carriage stand on the opposite side of the road has become a taxi stand but many of the rambling old bungalows exist as reminders of a bygone age. And yet 30 years ago Ludlow Castle was very much there with its turrets dreaming of the Raj and its majestic walls hiding the secrets of the club where the sahibs and memsahibs enjoyed their evenings after the sun had set on a hard day.

There was Diana Baby who sang to her lover on the piano, softly though, so as not to rock the hall, and there was Henry Sahib who drank whisky-soda and played the violin when the year ended to the strains of Auld Lang Syne and his friend, Holly the tall one, forever loitering with his girlfriend in the bushes, unmindful of the *missibaba* who sometimes cried quietly for the sahib who had left her. The wet handkerchief in her hand was the only evidence that she pined for someone whenever the Firangi company was making merry. But the biggest attraction was Denniese, the magistrate's daughter who wore the prettiest frocks and broke many a heart because she would not go steady with anyone.

They used to come in horse-driven carriages, racing down from the fort or beyond to play bridge or billiards, drink, talk, dine and dance in the huge chandeliered rooms which once served as the office of the Commissioner. The carriages were parked in the stand where the grooms used to sit huddled, building up or destroying the reputations of their sahibs at will; while those worthies, some with their sweethearts, strolled towards Rajpur Road to enjoy a few moments of bliss.

Inside the club people were engrossed in their own affairs though some of the nosey ones did not fail to notice the absence of the courting couples. But they were back by the time the *khansamas* laid out the dinner on occasions when feasting countinued till late at night and the ladies were specially invited to what was essentially a gentlemen's club. Christmas, of course, was one such occasion, and so were New Year's Eve and Easter. Later at night the sahibs escorted the memsahibs back home, though many of them were so tipsy that they had to be supported by the syce.

Those times are over and few remember Ludlow Castle or the defunct Bombay House of old Lewis, but still Raj Niwas Marg, where the Lieutenant-Governor resides, has the charm of a past age when life was much more leisurely than now and one had the time to stand and stare at the girls coming in their fancy ballroom dresses. They talk about those times in the bungalows along the road, where tales in the servants' quarters are passed on from father to son. The Delhi Club moved out of the area long ago to various places, last of all to a site opposite Willingdon Hospital. That building too is now on the verge of being demolished. But who can demolish gossip?

43

Grotto of Our Lady

The grotto outside the Cathedral of the Sacred Heart, where Pope John Paul II planted a sapling, is a venerated spot. Built by the late philanthropist Anthony Demello it is a replica of the shrine at Lourdes, in France, where the Virgin Mary appeared to a peasant girl named Bernadette on a rocky eminence. For those who cannot go for a pilgrimage to the original grotto, this is the place to make vows and light candles. People do so in large numbers on Sundays and feast days. The shrine depicts a hill with a hollow in the centre where a statue of the Virgin stands with folded hands. The fingers are slender and well shaped, but it is the comely face and expressive eyes that leave one spellbound. The Virgin is trampling the devil, depicted as the serpent, with her tender feet and at the same time casting a loving glance at the beholder. It is love and piety that it symbolizes and to gain these men, women and children throng the grotto.

Even when the church is closed, the grotto is open for all those who care to make their devotions. But late in the evening when nobody is around, an old bent woman is the sole supplicant at the shrine. She must be poor, for one can make that out from her clothes, and she is far advanced in years for her bent frame is proof of this. Still she carries two candles to merge her wishes with their amber light. They must be costing her a pretty penny but one supposes that's the only luxury she permits herself in her hand-to-mouth existence. What is the great urge that brings this woman here every evening? Is it to say the rosary after her day's work is done? She keeps kneeling for an hour or so, saying the beads with her eyes closed and her breath coming hard and fast in the gathering cold. Could it be that she prays for deliverance from her earthly existence? Or is it to seek a cure from some disease that she makes her vows? Maybe so, but seeing that she is a hardy old soul one wonders if she prays for someone else – a son, daughter or a grandchild.

Must be selfless devotion surely. One feels like walking up to the old woman and asking her what she seeks so intently. But that would be unwarranted interference in the personal life of someone. Overhearing the mumbled prayers too would amount to the same. Whatever be her thoughts, who can dare intrude into them? One can only watch and perchance pray, like the old man who visits the grotto every morning before attending mass.

The Virgin stands calm and unperturbed casting her benign glance at all those who come to ask favours. There is a peace which defies description enveloping the shrine; only the leaves of the overhead trees rustle in the evening breeze as the early stars peep into the grotto from the twilight sky. A nun on her way to the church might cross herself and bow her head to the Lily of the Valley, as Mary is called in the litany, or a passerby on the road outside might make a hasty salutation. The form that is the object of veneration does not lose its composure, for it is moulded after the artist's desire of divine tranquillity. But there is another form which is part of this picture: the bent old woman at her devotions, only her lips moving in the ritual incantation of 'Ave, Ave, Ave, Maria'.

44

Burning Day and Night

A lamp burns day and night in the Cathedral of the Sacred Heart. All days of the year, except Good Friday when it is extinguished. The sanctuary lamp is a reminder of divine presence. There was a time when an oil lamp burnt here, replenished every day by the sacristan, but now it is an electric one, mounted atop an old brass holder, suspended from the ceiling, which would be the delight of any antiquarian.

The church fills up with devotees every day and few think of the lamp that hangs opposite a giant painting of the Last Supper, with life-like personages in ancient Jewish robes and bearded according to their ages. Some have hoary beards and some well-maintained ones which show the youthfulness of their faces. The best of course is that of Christ who seems to be looking directly at the lamp. However, the truth is that those depicted in this painting are the priests who were serving during the building of the Church. A novel tribute to their labours.

The church was built by the Italian Friars Minor Capuchin, the order of monks in charge of the Agra Archdiocese from the middle of the 19th century to the middle of the 20th. Delhi then was controlled by the same Archbishop right up to Shimla.

The Sacred Heart Church is built partly on the lines of the Cathedral of the Immaculate Conception at Agra, which however is far bigger and with a belfry that can be seen from as far away as the Taj. It is a landmark of the city, the bells sounding the Angelus thrice a day – morning, noon and evening, besides the joy peals on Sundays and feast days.

The church at Delhi does not have such a prominent belfry, nor does it have a facade decorated with statues of as many saints as the one at Agra, but there are other characteristics which are outstanding, especially

Lamp burning day and night between two angels

the wide nave, shaped like a ship, as the church has to carry its devotees through the storms of life. There are pigeons living in the ventilators and sparrows too which dart in and out avoiding the lamp.

There is a certain solemnity about this symbol, a feature of all Catholic churches. The belief is that it will be finally put off at the end of the world when an all-pervading divine light will illumine the Eternal City so that one need not go to any special place to pray – a kindly light amidst the mundane. Until such time the sanctuary lamp would keep shining day and night.

45

Sari for the Virgin

A new *sari* is offered to the replica of the statue of our Lady of Velankanni at the Sacred Heart Cathedral whenever the wish of a devotee is fulfilled. This is in keeping with the tradition of Velankanni, in Nagapatnam, where the original shrine of the miraculous mother of Christ is situated.

The Virgin is said to have appeared to a lame boy and also to medieval Portuguese sailors whose ship was about to sink in a storm. Fearing the worst in the tempest the terrified men sought the intercession of the Virgin and behold, the storm ceased and their ship anchored safely.

The grateful sailors built a church which has since become a basilica, where people not only from India but also from abroad come to seek favours.

The statue at the Cathedral (one of the two icons in New Delhi) was installed to fulfil a long-standing demand of local Catholics who could not go all the way to Velankanni in the diocese of Tanjore. But its popularity surpasses that of all other statues. Flower-bedecked and with candles burning all around it, the Virgin looks resplendent in a new *sari* nearly every week. Foreigners coming to attend mass are also attracted by this sight, denied to them in their own land. Incidentally, there is a Velankanni shrine near Khan Market to which South Indians flock on Saturdays. Ask Jasmine Jose and she'll swear her sister got married thanks to Velankanni Mata.

The Virgin is generally portrayed in robes of the Renaissance period, blue and white being the most common colours – blue for the lady of the sky and the white for purity. This was the conception of Italian artists even though Mary was only the wife of an Israeli carpenter, whose garments were far from regal.

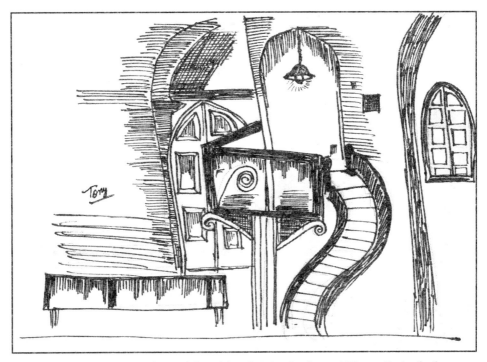

An artist's conception of the old pulpit in the Sacred Heart Cathedral

In India there are only two statues which depict the Virgin wearing a *sari* – Our Lady of Velankanni and the icon at Agra which is said to have been buried under the doorway of the Agra Fort on the orders of Aurangzeb.

The icon was unearthed mysteriously and now adorns the special altar outside Akbar's Church. In it the Virgin is shown wearing shoes, though everywhere else she is depicted barefoot. However, the Velankanni statue is unique in that a *sari* is actually draped around it. A strange custom at a strange shrine!

EUROPEAN LEGACY

46

Sikandar Sahib

'Hansi' is the place to which Balban had been forced to retire in AD 1253 because of court intrigues. That was during the Slave Sultanate. Balban came back from retirement and virtually ruled for 33 years. Students of history still remember the stern old man who beat back the Mongol invaders time and again despite the loss of his eldest son. Many centuries later Hansi became the retreat of Lt.-Col. James Skinner, who formed the famous Skinner's Horse and built the beautiful church in Kashmere Gate, Delhi. The old Skinner house still exists in Hansi, Haryana, where Brig. Michael Skinner was the chief representative of the Christian branch of the family till his death a few years ago.

The Skinner story is a well known one. James Skinner, the son of a Scot father and a Rajput mother, was born in 1778 at Calcutta. His father, Ulysses was in the service of the East India Company. When James was 12 years old his mother committed suicide and at the age of 16 he left home and came all the way to meet Benoit de Boigne, the French commander of the forces of Maharaja Scindia. His ancestry, which could be traced to the Skyners who served William the Conqueror, was something which greatly impressed de Boigne and he took James under his protection.

The boy did not betray the trust reposed in him and acquitted himself well in many skirmishes. The turning point came at the Battle of Uniara where he was wounded and left for dead. For three days he lay among the slain, praying that if God spared his life he would never fight again and build a church to perpetuate his vow. A cobbler's wife looking for valuables among the dead found that one of them was still alive and revived the young man. That was how James's life was saved.

St. James Church built by Skinner

Skinner honoured the woman as his mother till she lived and later also built the pledged church, but he never quit fighting. He formed an irregular cavalry known as the Yellow Boys, who were a dreaded lot, and virtually made him the most famous mercenary leader in North India. During Lord Lake's campaign in 1803 Skinner was much sought after by the British and eventually Lake succeeded in winning over the allegiance of the soldier of fortune. In 1815, the Marquess of Hastings watched with admiration the skill of the Yellow Boys in action. Still a commision in the British Army was denied to James and his brother Robert, who was the leader of another band of irregulars, because of their mixed parentage.

Undaunted, the Yellow Boys continued to fight under Sikandar Sahib, as James is known, with their cry 'Himmat-i-Mardan, Madat-i-Khuda' (courage of man and help of God). In 1828 James was finally given the rank of Lieutenant-Colonel and his brother that of Major.

But Robert blew out his brains soon after killing his wife and her paramour. James lived on till 1841, smoking the *hookah* at his country retreat and generally pleased with his accomplishments. Surrounded by his admirers (among whom he missed William Fraser, late British Agent at the Moghul Court), Skinner gave the impression of a *nawab* seated on Persian carpets at Hansi.

His descendants are now to be found in London, Glasgow and Sydney, besides India. Skinner's eldest son from a Muslim wife and his descendants lived in Meerut. But the Hansi estate was until recently run by the late Brig. Michael Skinner, who retired as commander of Skinner's Horse, now a mechanized unit of the Indian Army. He and his wife, also a Skinner descendant, owned land in Hansi and divided their time between their retreat and the family house at Mussoorie. There are portraits of his ancestors on the walls, the pride of place being taken by those of James Skinner, to whom Michael bore a close resemblance. His grandmother, Asharfi Begum once lived at Hansi and tended the garden, which is not so well maintained now. But the verandahs, hall and bedrooms still whisper tales of the romantic times when Sikandar Sahib held sway.

That James's descendants continued to amaze the British is borne out by this entry recorded in the journal kept by Herbert John Maynard, Commissioner of Hissar in 1887, which has been published in the *Chowkidar*, a quarterly of the British Association for Cemeteries in South Asia, courtesy a descendant of Mr. Maynard who now lives in Devon, England.

On the morning of New Year's eve, 1887, young Mr. Maynard, Commissioner of Hissar, was handed a card with the inscription 'Alexander van Cortlandt Skinner – Captain, 1st Bengal Cavalry'. Maynard wrote:

> I was a trifle surprised knowing that no troops are quartered near here, but my surprise was increased when I saw the owner of the card. He was the most complete mixture of native and Englishman that I have ever seen. His colour was jet; his features were massive and like those of a European; his legs were cased in the neatest of hunting boots, and his clothes were of the English pattern, his head was covered by a gorgeous turban. He spoke English perfectly and with obvious knowledge of the slang and conversational expressions and for part of the time he discoursed of hunting and shooting like a young country gentleman. Then he announced that he had come to pay his respects to me. His grandfather, Colonel Skinner served under the English, after having been employed by some native prince, and received large estates as a reward for work done before the Mutiny. This man lives on a part of these estates, in a fine house at Hansi, with a native wife. His commission is an honorary one, given him by the Prince of Wales. I took him out to see him off. He mounted a fine camel and rode out of the gate towards the city.

Incidentally, Alexander had first married an English woman but he left her after she accused him of cruelty. The lady attributed this to her husband's Scottish origin.

47

Muztar and Azad

Benjamin Montrose 'Muztar' was the pupil of Ustad Daagh Dehlvi. A scion of the European Montrose family, which came to India in the 18th century, Muztar wrote some very pithy verse. But the more interesting thing about him is this story:

One day when he was returning from the Kalhari or tavern, he saw a white horse nibbling grass before a cemetery gate. Liquor does not intoxicate only. It also opens lips which have remained sealed for long. Muztar began reciting his compositions. Ghalib's elegy on the death of his nephew, Nawab Zainul Abdin Arif, suddenly came to his mind, for Arif had died young, like Keats.

Even as he lingered the cemetery gate opened and out of it emerged an old man. The man started staring at him. His eyes glowing. He opened his mouth and emitted a bluish flame.

Muztar thought that the old man was trying to force his willpower on him. He felt quite sober now and began to wonder if what confronted him was a phantom. The thought had hardly struck him when the old man mounted the white horse and rode away into nothingness.

Something zoomed past Muztar's ear. It was a bat and it made for the neighbouring tree from which an owl suddenly began to hoot. The message of the night was clear. He wiped his forehead and hurried home.

Was there really such an incident that scared Muztar out of his wits? Well that is what the old tale says. Muztar survived many more years but his Ustad, Daagh, and friend Alexander Heatherley Azad, predeceased him.

Alexander Heatherley Azad (1829-1861) was probably one of the best exponents of shairi, having attained complete mastery of Urdu poetry.

He was the pupil of Arif, the nephew whose death Ghalib had mourned. He has left a complete 'dewan' which contains *ghazals*, *qitas*, chronograms, a short *masnavi* and, a poetical epistle.

His poems are of a very high order and show him to be a remarkable master of Urdu. This is all the more creditable because the poet died aged 32. He is certainly in the first rank of Anglo-Indian poets who wrote Urdu verse, says his descendant George Heatherley, on his annual visit to the Capital from Perth, where he has settled down.

Muztar

The Heatherleys, like the Montrose family, also came to India in the 18th century. George Heatherley, now 85 but still a very active man who belies his age, has culled the following information about his remarkable family.

> Its ancestor, James Heatherley, came of English stock. There were some very valuable records of the family and appreciations of meritorious services rendered by the ancestors to Alwar, Bharatpur, Jhajhar, Khetri (Jaipur) and other States. Unfortunately these records were destroyed in a fire, including the manuscript of *Diwan-e-Azad* in the handwriting of the poet.

> James Heatherley died in England about 1799. He was the son of Baron Heatherley of Heatherely House, Salisbury, England. He was a captain in the Royal Navy and came out to India in 1789 with his wife, son and daughter. Son also named James. His intention was to start a career in India and with this in mind returned to England, leaving his wife, son James and daughter in Calcutta, in order to resign from his service, dispose of his property, and eventually settling down in India on his return. He, however, died of an epileptic fit shortly after his arrival in England.

> James Heatherley Jr. was born in England. Resulting from his father's sudden demise, James and his mother found themselves stranded in Calcutta. The sister having died meanwhile. He was sent to school with the help of a business firm, Messrs Colvin & Horeley. In 1801, at the age of fourteen he worked in the office of Executive Engineer, Fort William,

Calcutta. He also worked under Mr. Fortisque in the Commissioner's Office, Bareilly. He was transferred to the Collector's Office, Moradabad, and was there from 1803 to 1805. For six months he was employed under Colonel Ochterlony in Delhi Residency. From 1805 to 1821 he served in the Collector's Office, Meerut. He was translator of Persian in Sadar Board, Meerut, from 1824 to 1829. He was also in the Commissioner's Office, Meerut, from 1829 to 1833.

He retired after 30 years of Government Service in 1833 and on the recommendation of Mr. Blake, Assistant, and Mr. Fraser, Agent to the Governor-General at Delhi, took up service in Jhajhar State. In 1857, he was taken prisoner by the British owing to a rising of State forces and was released, given protection by Captain Lawrence and pensioned in April 1858 by order of the Government. He died at Meerut on 18th December 1859. James was married to Miss Wollands, daughter of James Wollands.

Thomas Heatherley (son of James) commenced his career in his father's lifetime in the service of the *Nawab* of Jhajhar. In 1855 Sir Henry Lawrence took him over and sent him to different places connected with the Revenue Department. In 1862 he was Deputy Collector and retired as Head of the Land Revenue Dept. and given a certificate of Meritorious Service by Command of His Excellency the Viceroy of the Empress of India dated 1st January 1877. He died in Meerut in 1891.

George Heatherley (son of James). He served in various capacities, Superintendent of Jails; Inspector of Schools; Municipal Commissioner. He was married to Miss Bella Rustle and had two children – Alice and a son, Leslie. Alice married Thomas Grissonne on 20th August 1888. George died in Delhi in 1901.

Henry Heatherley (another son of James). He was employed as Assistant Private Secretary to H.H. Maharaja Mangal Singh of Alwar. After the death of the Maharaja he served in various capacities before coming to Delhi in 1900 to settle down there at the request of his sister, Mrs. Jane Skinner. Henry died in Delhi in 1924.

Miss Jane Heatherley, daughter of James, was married to James Cousins Skinner, Rais of Delhi, on 15th Novermber 1869. He presented Queen Victoria's statue to Delhi Municipality, which stood in Chandni Chowk (up to a few years ago). J.C. Skinner was the grandson of Colonel James Skinner, founder of "Skinner's Horse" (The Yellow Boys) and builder of St. James' Church, Kashmere Gate, Delhi.

George Heatherley Jr., named after one of his ancestors, has a complete family tree which shows his ancestry. He is looking for the works of Alexander Heatherley Azad. There are some in the libraries. But what about Benjamin Montrose Muztar? Can somebody trace all his works?

48

Armenian Connexion

The visit of the former Armenian President, Levon Der Petrossian, was a reminder of the age-old ties between India and Armenia, two countries where the Aryan influence predominated. As early as the Roman times there was a flourishing trade between India and Armenia.

Armenia is an ancient country which has been regarded as "the doorway between East and West." Mount Ararat, where Noah's Ark rested after the Deluge, was in the present Turkish part of Armenia and it was there that those who were saved from the great flood along with the patriarch settled down to create a new world. In later times the Jewish influence made its impact on the population under the Assyrian and Babylonian kings who had carried away the Jews from their homeland into captivity. It was, therefore, natural for Christianity to take root there in its initial days.

The story about King Abgar having been in correspondence with Christ may be the stuff of legends as also the belief that the two Apostles, Bartholomew and Thaddeaus (also known as Jude) visited the region. For that matter, it is believed by some that St. Bartholomew came to India by way of Kashmir at about the same time as St. Thomas arrived in South India. So there could be some substance in the belief of the Armenians because the Apostles did preach in Syria.

However, it is recorded that King Tridates was baptized by George the Illuminator in about AD 250 and that Armenian bishops, at least two of them, were present at the Council of Nice which had such a great bearing on Christian belief. It is worth mentioning, however, that the old beliefs of the Armenians were incorporated into the Church for quite a long time. Animals were sacrificed in the church porch before the celebration of the Eucharest. The meat was eaten at what were known as the preparatory sacrifices at a time when Akbar the Great was ruling Hindustan. The Armenians had started coming to the Moghul empire some years before the invasion of their country.

They found the hospitality that they needed and built churches in Delhi, which however do not exist now. At Agra also they built a chapel and the son of a nobleman, Mirza Zulquarnain, was brought up by Akbar. He was later to become the head of the salt works at Samhbar.

The Mirza is known as the father of Christianity in North India because it was during his time that the cross and the crescent met in the Moghul capital.

Mirza Zulquarnain's palace occupied the land where the British later built the Agra Central Prison, which in recent times has made way for the ambitious shopping project known as Sanjay Place. It was on this piece of land that a cathedral was erected by the Capuchins 200 years later. The Armenians planted olive trees, one of which still survives near Akbar's church. Their mystical cross was used as an emblem on even residential buildings. It is said that during Akbar's time after Mass the sick members of the congregation drank of the water in which earlier a crucifix had been bathed. It was supposed to cure patients, or so the belief went.

In the Martyrs' Cemetery at Agra are the graves of many Armenians which look like Muslim graves with Persian inscriptions. One of the graves, that of the saintly Armenian merchant, Khwaja Mortiniphas is still venerated. Some say he was related to the Bishop of Tabriz and became a hermit in later life after giving all his wealth to the poor.

In Delhi the most famous Armenian tomb is that of Sarmad Shaheed at the foot of the Jama Masjid. Sarmad, an Armenian Jew who had come as a merchant trading in precious stones, converted to Islam and became a mystic. He was beheaded as a heretic by Aurangzeb. The last of the Armenians in Agra died in 1920, though one remembers a boy called Arathoon who was the best shadow-boxer in school during the war years. But he was from Calcutta where the community flourished. Its imposing church there was visited by the Armenian President. So the old Armenian connexion continues.

49

The French Connexion

Bibi Juliana-ki-Sarai in Delhi was an important halting place in Moghul India. Caravans stopped there and so did the lone traveller, mounted or footing it out. The journeys were much longer in medieval times because the horse was the fastest mode of conveyance. It was on horseback that Akbar reached Gujarat in 11 days to quell the rebellion by his half-brother Mirza Hakim. The rebels naturally had not expected the emperor to arrive 'so soon' because their spies had reported that he was making merry at Fatehpur Sikri.

Juliana and her sister Maria were Portuguese and had been sent to the Moghul court as maids of honour. Juliana spent time in Delhi too where she built a *sarai*; though after her marriage to Philippe Bourbon she mostly stayed near the Karbala in Agra where stood the mansions of the Europeans – Spanish, Flemish, English and Dutch, besides Portuguese and French. But no trace remains of them now.

However in the nearby Martyrs' Cemetery one traced the mausoleum of Bibi Amiana (Juliana's niece) amidst the tombs of the Armenians, who flourished as a community in Agra during the reigns of Akbar, Jehangir and Shah Jehan – and even later for the last of them died there in 1920. On one side is the Ellis Memorial. Below the platform are the graves of the Armenian Cestans, near those of the descendants of Colonel Salvador Smith of the Gwalior Army. A hedge separates these from the Bibi's mausoleum. But the *Ashoka* tree that grew near it for many years was uprooted in a storm in 1991.

One sits outside the mausoleum and wonders about the times in which Bibi Juliana lived. The history of the Bourbons in Agra is mostly confined to the annals of the Archdiocese or the memory of the old inhabitants.

The grave in the mausoleum (Juliana and her husband are buried at Akbar's church a few kilometres away) has a Persian inscription much of which has been obliterated by time. Sometimes the cemetery gardener sleeps in the burial chamber and sometimes the cat that prowls about the place. The *maqbara*, however, is still intact and looks like a discarded mosque from a distance.

Incidentally, Bibi Juliana was not only in-charge of the harem but also the Moghul hospital and the department of endowments. She was also the patron of orphan and exploited girls. Many regard her as the precursor of Florence Nightingale for she was a source of great solace to the sick, the infirm and the destitute. Wherever the Bibi went there was light, happiness and plenty. The *sarai* in Delhi was a symbol of her philanthropy. (But the one in Masihgarh was built in the 17th century by her namesake Donna Juliana Diaz da Costa).

From Bibi Juliana's union with Jeane Philippe, blessed by Akbar's chief queen, came into being a whole clan of Indian Bourbons. Their descendants served the latter Moghuls. But when Nadir Shah invaded Delhi and carried out a wholesale massacre in 1739, the Bourbons began to feel insecure. Soon after they left the kingdom of Mohammad Shah Rangila in response to an invitation from the Raja of Narwar, in all 300 souls descended from just one man. But the Bourbons were ill-treated by the Raja and then one night many of them were massacred.

The remainder sought refuge in Bhopal in 1758, where they later took up employment with the *nawab*, mostly in the army, with Salvador Bourbon helping to organize the troops against the onslaughts of the Marathas. It is worth mentioning that Narwar rhymes with Navarre, the royal house to which Philippe Bourbon and Henry IV belonged. The latter was assassinated in 1610, five years after the death of Akbar.

In Bhopal the Bourbons took up names like Innayat Masih, Shamshad Masih, Shahzad Masih and Mumtaz Masih which, though not actually Muslim, nevertheless were more in keeping with the milieu of their new place of habitation. Isabella, the wife of Balthazar Bourbon, Prime Minister of Bhopal up to 1829, was known as Madam Dulhan. She wore oriental clothes, observed *purdah* even while going to church and smoked the *hookah*, like any other begum of the time.

Her descendants intermarried with Indo-Europeans in other princely States, including those in Rajputana or with Anglo-Indians. Some wrote Urdu poetry too and some whiled away their time in mirth and song, powered by strong drink. But with the break-up of the princely houses and the abolition of *zamindari* the Bourbons fell on bad days again.

The scion of the family in Bhopal now is a work-a-day man, Balthazar Napoleon Bourbon III, who lives in a house-cum-school with his wife, and three children. The wife, Elisha, runs the school and they have some ancestral land too but the days of glory are over. Or so one thought until the recent revelation that Balthazar is now regarded by Prince Michael of Greece, and another Bourbon, the King of Spain, as No. 1 claimant to the French throne.

The saga of Jeane Philippe Bourbon, however, survies both in Bhopal and Agra, though the family does not seem to have left much trace in Delhi, except for the fact that they were known as Francisi Sirdars right up to the time of Mohammand Shah (1719-1748).

The Bourbons guarded their women zealously and it hardly mattered to the emperor, known as Rangila Pia (the colourful consort), when they decided to seek their fortune elsewhere.

50

Good Old Halls of the Raj

Many buildings came into existence in Delhi during the days of the Raj. Probably the most famous among them was Metcalfe House built by Sir Thomas Metcalfe, which now houses the offices of the DRDO. His brother, Sir (later Lord) Charles Metcalfe built the Metcalfe Testimonial at Agra, which was destroyed in a fire. Metcalfe House too was destroyed during the 'Mutiny' but was rebuilt. Atal Hall in Bazar Sita Ram was not a British building but the ancestral residence of Kamla Kaul, who married Pandit Nehru. In Chandni Chowk the Town Hall was built as an office complex in 1863. Hallingar Hall was an Anglo-Indian creation. And what a colourful place it was!

The dining hall of Metcalfe House (Matka Kothi) vibrated with life at the parties thrown by Sir Thomas. His guests included the British officers posted in Delhi to keep an eye on the Moghul court. But his predecessor, William Fraser, as chief of the East India Company Residency used to think the Metcalfes a stuck-up lot and liked to keep to himself or enjoy the company of Col. James Skinner, who also happened to be his best friend.

Skinner's house in Mori Gate had a big hall too, where the parties were just as colourful. Fraser preferred the Hansi estate of Sikandar Sahib (as Skinner was known to his Indian troops). Among the weekend visitors to Hansi was Martin Sahib, a young man born about the time Fraser was murdered in 1835. He was later to build Hallingar Hall at Agra. Father used to recall that his son TBC Martin (Munna Baba) inherited it and lived there in the early 1920s. It is now part of a colony behind the civil courts. On the other side is the Martyrs' Cemetery dating back to Akbar's times and next to it the lodge built by Lady Doctor Ulrick. On the same road was the bungalow of Ball the magistrate (later occupied by the lawyer

Tavakalay) and a little further off the thatched cottage atop a hill where his son stayed.

Ball was quite an institution. The old man was around at the time of the 'Mutiny' and his son followed him into the magistracy. The daughter was an excellent dancer famed for her beauty. Now back to Hallinger Hall.

The elder Martin was a young man in 1858 and took part in the campaign against the Rani of Jhansi. He followed her closely into a *khaliyan* during her retreat, when she suddenly turned around and ordered him not to pursue her but to look for buried treasure as his reward. He found it all right in the barn and Mrs. McGuire used to tell the story by the fireside in after-years.

Hallinger Hall was built by Martin Sr. and it was a palatial building, compared by some yarn-spinners to the hall Heorot in Hrothgar's kingdom, in which Beowulf tackled the giant monster Grendel.

Hallinger Hall had no such visitations, but one of the first Xmas plays in North India, says T.S., was held here. Whatever memories there are of this hall survive only in old wives' tales. And the same may be said of the other halls. Metcalfe House Hall had a goodly collection of Napoleon's busts and other memorabilia of 'the Little Emperor' which were sent away to Mussoorie when the building was taken over by the government.

Sir Thomas Metcalfe was a great admirer of Napoleon, who happened to be his contemporary. The Metcalfes were Scottish and, unlike the English, did not regard the French emperor with disdain.

Atal Hall (like Haksar Haveli) is in a shambles as nobody was keen to preserve it, despite a much-publicised visit by Indira Gandhi. The Town Hall had a library and museum once before becoming a rabbit warren of a municipal office. There are however plans to restore it to its former grandeur. The Gospel Hall in Connaught Place is a miniature creation, but the earliest hall was the one thousand-pillared one of Alauddin Khilji at his now ruined city Siri. The Siri Fort auditorium is a reminder of sorts of Siri's lost glory. Incidentally, the most fabulous hall was the one built by Yudhishtira in Indraprastha. But that was in pre-historic times, when Delhi was yet to acquire the status of an imparial city.

Index